Contents

4

Acknowledgements

I would like to thank the following people and organisations, without whose help and support this book would not have been possible: Tower Hamlets Education Authority for funding my secondment in the spring and summer terms of 1991 to carry out the necessary reading and research, and staff, pupils and governors of Morpeth School in Tower Hamlets who have been willing 'guinea pigs' for many of the ideas represented herein. Staff at the Education Department of Cambridge University, where I was teacher associate, were gracious and helpful at all times: Professor David Hargreaves, Margaret Wilkin and Dr Martin Booth in particular.

I visited many places and interviewed many people in the course of my research and would like to record my indebtedness to them. First, all the mentors in the Tower Hamlets articled teacher scheme: Morag Robertson and Chris Julian, Kath Tideman, Ian Rouse, Paul Bonnell, Shanta Ayengar and Debbie Weston. Thanks also go to their headteachers, Chris Rose of the University of Greenwich and Geoff Binks, Poobie Naidoo, Rehana Alom and Robert Briscoe in Tower Hamlets.

In Oxfordshire I was given a warm welcome by Anna Pendry of the Department of Educational Studies and at the Cherwell School by the head, Martin Roberts, the mentor, Katherine Burn and the professional tutor, Kevin O'Reagan.

Thanks are also due to: Ian Hunt, then in the London Borough of Newham; Doris Rivalland of the NAHT; Elsa Dicks of NCVQ; Carol Baker, HMI; John Whittaker of the DES; Jackie Durrell and Margaret Alfrey of Christ Church College in Canterbury; Rod Knight of the University of Hertfordshire; Dr. Dennis Mongon of Hertfordshire LEA; Pat Heery of Roehampton Institute; Mike Farrell of South Bank University and Mike Fielding of Sussex University. The staff of my current school, Tong Upper School, in Bradford, have made revisions possible through their training activities. I am grateful to them.

Most of all I owe grateful thanks to Professor John Furlong, late of Cambridge and now in post at Swansea University, who officially supervised my efforts in the first half of 1991 (and thereafter unoffically), giving both encouragement and constructive criticism. The ideal mentor.

Foreword to the Second Edition

During the last few years, initial teacher training (ITT) in England and Wales has undergone major transformation. For example, the number of different possible 'routes' into the teaching profession has been considerably extended (Barrett *et al.*, 1992). In addition to conventional BEd degrees and PGCE courses, students can now choose from a wide range of shortened courses, conversion courses, and part-time courses. They can if they wish train to be a teacher anywhere in the country by enrolling with the Open University or they can choose routes which do not necessarily involve higher education at all. The Licensed Teacher scheme, for example, allows prospective teachers to be recruited directly to teaching posts and provided with 'on the job' training appropriate to their identified training needs; the School Centred Initial Teacher Training scheme (SCITT) (DFE, 1993d) allows consortia of schools rather than higher education institutions to become the 'lead bodies' in training schemes.

What all these 'new routes' have in common is a far greater role for schools in the training process than in the past. In the Licensed Teacher scheme and the SCITT scheme it is the school itself that has the principal responsibility for training; any involvement of higher education is secondary. But a greater role for schools is not simply something that is confined to new types of course. Throughout the last ten years the government has increasingly insisted that schools take a major role in all forms of ITT. As the most recent DFE Circular on secondary ITT (DFE, 1992a) states:

> The Government expects that partner schools and HEIs will exercise a joint responsibility for the planning and management of courses and the

selection, training and assessment of students. The balance of responsibilities will vary. Schools will have a leading responsibility for training students to teach their specialist subjects, to assess pupils and to manage classes; and for supervising students and assessing their competence in these respects. HEIs will be responsible for ensuring that courses meet the requirements for academic validation, presenting courses for accreditation, awarding qualifications to successful students and arranging student placements in more than one school. (para 14)

Background

The idea that schools should take a major role in the training process is not a new one. As long ago as 1944, the McNair Committee (McNair, 1944) appointed by the then Board of Education to look into the 'supply, recruitment and training of teachers', concluded that the key to more effective teacher training was to give the practical side of preparation greater weight. Specifically, McNair proposed that the staff in schools in which students were placed on teaching practice 'should be primarily responsible for directing and supervising [them]' (para 261). It was also suggested that in order to achieve more effective training, training institutions would have to 'relinquish a measure of responsibility in the training of their students' (para 270). But the McNair proposals fell on deaf ears and it has taken a further 50 years for such ideas to come to the forefront of educational policy.

In moving to a position where the vision set out by the McNair Committee may at last be achieved, it is possible to distinguish a number of different sources of pressure for change. The first has come from those inside the education service itself. For nearly 20 years now, a range of different professional groups (teacher educators, teacher unions, the CNAA, philosophers of education) have all been arguing, like the McNair Committee, that the key to more effective training is to give greater responsibility to schools (Wilkin, 1990). In most cases, what they have argued for are forms of 'partnership' between training institutions and schools, and a range of different models of school-based training have been developed.

A second impetus for change has come from political groups outside the education service. 'New Right' pressure groups, such as the Hillgate Group (Hillgate, 1989) and the Centre for Policy Studies (Lawlor, 1990), have mounted a sustained critique of initial training institutions and their 'monopoly' of the training process. Rather than arguing for partnership, many of these commentators have argued for the total abolition of institutionalised training with responsibility being entirely transferred to schools. Behind the 'New Right' critique has been concern about the character and quality of initial teacher training, a concern further fuelled by the government itself through the HMI and DFE. During the 1980s, these two bodies issued a vast array of research findings, inspection reports, consultation documents and directives, many of them implicitly and explicitly critical of existing approaches to teacher education (DES, 1983; DES, 1987; HMI, 1988).

As a result of this debate, throughout the last 12 years the government has taken a range of initiatives which have progressively increased the involvement of schools in the initial training process until now, as we have seen, they have at least equal responsibility to that of higher education.

To this increased involvement in initial teacher training must be added a growing responsibility for the delivery of school-based in-service training, the introduction of appraisal and an increased emphasis on support for newly qualified teachers. It is clear that in the future *all* schools will have to see themselves as 'training schools', taking a key role in the professional development of their staff throughout their teaching career.

The way forward

Simply because schools have had these new responsibilities thrust upon them does not necessarily mean that they are currently well prepared to make an effective contribution to the training process. The 1992 HMI report on school-based initial teacher training suggested that while there had been very considerable improvements in the quality of institution-based training, there was still considerable scope for improvement in the quality of many aspects of school-based work.

What, then, are the key issues that must be addressed if schools are to become more effective in the training process? Three issues would seem to be particularly important.

Institutional needs

First, senior staff need to recognise that, if it is to be effective, training is a whole-school issue, not merely the responsibility of one or two designated 'mentors'. This point was explicitly recognised by Kenneth Clarke who, as Secretary of State for Education in 1992, first announced the move to school-based training:

> I find the concept of the 'mentor' teacher with a particular responsibility for a student or group of students an attractive one. At the same time it should be developed within a policy of training which involves the whole school . . . [T]he arrangements which each school makes will reflect the commitment of heads and governors and should be a feature of the school's development plan. (Clarke, 1992:8)

Senior staff therefore need to develop an awareness of how effective their school is as a whole in discharging its current training responsibilities – perhaps, as Shaw suggests, undertaking an 'audit' of current practice to identify strengths, weaknesses and development needs.

Mentor training

A second need concerns mentor training. Far too few teachers are currently trained for their mentoring responsibilities. Effective mentoring makes new professional demands on teachers. They need to have a detailed understanding of their responsibilities within a particular training scheme, have the appropriate interpersonal skills for working with adult learners, develop an appropriate 'language' in order to articulate their professional knowledge in relation to a wide range of issues of professional practice, and develop a repertoire of supervisory strategies appropriate for different stages of student development (Furlong and Maynard, 1995). Again, Shaw presents practical help and guidance in how to establish effective forms of mentor training.

Establishing effective partnership

However committed schools are to developing themselves as training institutions, most consider that their primary function is to teach pupils, not to teach teachers or students. As a result, no matter how well developed the institution, however well trained the mentors, most schools recognise that they cannot provide for all of the professional development needs of their staff. Developing effective training therefore means working in 'partnership' with outside agencies such as LEAs and training institutions.

Over the last 15 years or so a number of investigations have been carried out into different forms of school-based initial training (Lacey, 1977; Furlong *et al.*, 1988; Benton, 1990). Despite important differences between these studies, all of them agree that effective training is dependent on students being exposed to a variety of different forms of professional knowledge. Some of that knowledge can only be acquired through direct practical experience in schools; other knowledge of a more reflective and analytical kind is more frequently encountered in higher education institutions. The challenge of effective training is how to design a course which encourages students to integrate different forms of professional knowledge with their practical work in school. If that integration is to be achieved, it is dependent on schools themselves having a clear vision of the different elements of the training process and their contribution to it. It may be obvious but it needs to be said that partnership can only work if roles, responsibilities and patterns of communication are clear. Once again, Shaw provides practical advice on how to assess existing partnership arrangements and establish effective forms of collaboration.

If these then, are the needs for the development of more effective school-based training, this book will provide a vitally important resource to all heads and senior teachers. It will, I believe, prove equally valuable for those who have worked in the area of professional development for many years, and for those about to begin. It offers a practical and thoughtful guide on how schools can maximise their training role.

As Shaw herself notes, taking training more seriously not only helps produce more effective teachers, it also encourages the school to be more reflective about its own ways of working. The promise of good school-based training held out by Shaw is one of better-trained teachers and more effective schools. As such, she suggests, it is a vitally important resource in the struggle of schools to improve the learning experience of our children.

Professor John Furlong
Department of Education
University of Wales, Swansea
March 1995

Chapter 1

Why Schools Should Concentrate on Teacher Training

There are two main reasons why schools should concentrate on teacher training. The first relates to factors external to the school: social, economic and political changes. The second is an internal factor: the questions of the development of the 'reflective school' and of 'school improvement'. First, however, let us define what we mean by teacher training.

Defining teacher training

The need for a unified approach

A coherent approach to training in schools is in part prevented by the common assumption that teacher training takes place in separate 'compartments' not linked in any way. Once initial training is over the new teacher has begun the induction period as a completely separate step, with no reference to training already carried out, nor to the individual strengths and weaknesses identified during that period. It is strange that this division of teacher training into separate stages persists, as it has long been seen as undesirable. In 1941, in a memorandum to the Association of Directors and Secretaries for Education, Henry Morris, the founder of the Community College movement wrote: 'We have somehow to find a method of ensuring that the education and technical training of teachers goes on throughout their careers . . .' (Ree, 1973).

The major argument of the James report of 1972 which studied all aspects of teacher training was that the education and training of teachers 'should be seen as falling into three consecutive stages or "cycles": the first, personal education, the second pre-service training and induction, the third, inservice education and training' (DES, 1972, 1.9, 6.5). This proposed the merging of initial training and the probationary period into one discrete stage. Although many of the recommendations of this report were implemented, this first one had until recently been largely ignored.

In a letter to local authorities and other interested parties setting out the consultation period relating to the abolition of the statutory schoolteacher probation, the DES commented in 1991: '[The Secretary of State] wishes to reinforce the continuity between initial training, induction and career-long professional development . . .' (DES, 1991f). The letter, like this book, uses the term 'training' to embrace initial teacher training, induction training and on-going professional development.

It also draws a clear link between the training of teachers and their appraisal. Teacher appraisal is now a reality. In its report on appraisal, ACAS recommended that appraisal should be understood 'not as a series of perfunctory periodic events, but as a continuous and systematic process intended to help individual teachers with their professional development and career planning' (DES, 1989e). This statement can be applied equally to the continuous process of teacher training.

The training continuum

Teacher training can be expressed as a continuum:

Personal experience as a school pupil → Initial training → Induction period→ Staff development→ Appraisal → Further staff development.

In this book the term 'teacher training' can mean all the stages listed above and we shall attempt to clarify the specific training context where necessary.

Initial training

For instance, *initial teacher training* in secondary schools can consist of the traditional routes through the two-, three- or four-year Bachelor of Education (BEd) qualification, the one-year Post Graduate Certificate of Education (PGCE) or the recently ended two-year school-based PGCE known as the Articled Teacher Scheme. Other forms of initial teacher training include the Licensed Teacher scheme, the 'fast track' route for teachers trained overseas, school-centred initial training and the registered teacher scheme for the training of technology teachers by City Technology Colleges (CTCs), City Colleges for the Technology of the Arts (CCTAs) and their partners.

Induction training

The statutory probationary period for newly trained teachers disappeared in September 1992. The lack of a statutory period of *induction training* does not lessen the needs of young teachers for guidance and support in the early years of their careers. Indeed the consultation document specifically referred to non-statutory guidelines for probation and to the need for new and improved induction schemes developed jointly by LEAs, teacher training institutions and schools (DES, 1991f). It also pinpointed the importance of the first two years of a teacher's career in highlighting strengths and weaknesses and the eventual dismissal of those who fail to respond to training with an improved performance in the classroom. It is now a statutory requirement for head teachers to ensure that newly qualified teachers have access to adequate support in their first year of service (DFE, 1994a, 32.8.3)

Schools concerned with effective teaching and quality control will therefore continue to provide a period of induction training for teachers in their first years of teaching. Of course, induction is also needed for teachers who change schools at any time in their career.

Staff development

This begins on the first day as a teacher and continues to the last day. It encompasses the first-hand experience learned at the 'chalk face', courses and in-service training attended by the individual, professional reading, good practice in teaching and management learnt from other colleagues both consciously and unconsciously, as well as individual and team staff development gained in meetings with other teachers to discuss matters of common concern. All these processes serve to increase a teacher's expertise.

Appraisal

The *appraisal* cycle not only provides a statement of a teacher's effectiveness in delivering the agreed elements of a job description but also helps the appraisee and the appraiser to identify the staff development and training needs of the person being appraised. If it does not then lead to further staff development and enhanced performance the appraisal cycle is a meaningless exercise.

The 'reflective practitioner' should see the move to the next stage as a progression to greater expertise, offering the opportunity to focus in a formative way on areas of professional skill which need further development.

School-based teacher training is certainly not a new phenomenon. The apprenticeship model or 'sitting with Nellie' dates back to the earliest days of schooling for the working classes in the late eighteenth century (Wragg, in Booth, *et al.*, 1990, p 25). In this century there has never been more interest in all types of school-based training than at the present time. There are several reasons for this which are discussed below, relating mainly to social, economic and political factors which, although often difficult to manage for educationalists at all levels, have generated both a fruitful debate about the relationship between theory and practice, and new forms of partnership between academics and practitioners which can only be to the benefit of all involved.

External factors

This section examines why there has been a resurgence of interest in school-based initial teacher training, induction training and staff development. It begins by looking at the effects of the high teacher turnover in the 1980s on recruitment and retention policies and on pupil achievement. It then describes some reforms and innovations in initial training course patterns following political and legislative changes arising both out of teacher shortages and the desire to shift the balance in initial training from the theoretical to the practical, apprenticeship-type model.

The effect of teacher shortages on pupil achievement

Acute teacher shortages peaked in the late 1980s and although they have been felt most severely in the south-east and in inner city areas there has been considerable impact in the rest of the country in certain subjects such as mathematics, modern languages, science and music. Some traces of these subject shortages still remain.

HMI, in their report on Hackney schools (DES, 1990d) stated that the results of high teacher turnover, including untaught classes, the extensive use of supply teachers and staff trained overseas as well as the need for proper staff development in schools, had had a negative effect on pupil achievement and teacher performance. Frequent changes had signalled a need for clearly articulated policies underpinned by high aspirations.

An earlier report (DES, 1989d) showed that in the schools visited, all of which had a high teacher turnover:

> even when individual lessons were effectively taught the cumulative effect of the staffing turnover had a significant effect on the total pattern of learning in some instances. Where there had been a succession of teachers the planning of work had frequently been neglected, and records were incomplete. . . . Expectations were low . . . and there was frequently a noisy atmosphere, poor motivation and poor relationships (p 5).

HMI also noted that 'There were teachers whose qualifications and experience were not well matched to the demands of the curriculum . . .' (p 6).

These findings confirm the conclusion which simple common sense makes inevitable: that the frequent changes of teacher, the extensive use of supply teachers, the shortage of subject specialists, the lack of continuity in the classroom and the stresses that these place on the remaining staff cohort must render the primordial task of the school, helping pupils to fulfil their potential, extremely difficult. Pupils are faced with varying expectations of work and behaviour and their motivation suffers.

While the problems described above relate primarily to inner city schools, all schools must plan to set out clearly their expectations of teacher performance, curriculum delivery and staff training. A coherent and flexible package of induction and training will efficiently remove some of the constraints which prevent pupils from receiving as consistent an education as may be possible under the circumstances.

Measures aimed at reducing the high teacher turnover and teacher shortages

A discussion of the reasons for these shortages is irrelevant to this study but the effect of them has been to force government, LEAs and individual schools to concentrate efforts on effective strategies for the recruitment and retention of teachers, some of which are briefly described below. Inevitably, this has had implications for teacher training institutions who are also players on the field of teacher recruitment.

Recruitment of teachers: alternative routes

A very significant consequence of teacher shortages was the creation of alternative routes into teaching by government legislation: the recruitment of overseas trained teachers, encouragement to return to teaching for those who have left the profession as well as the Licensed Teachers' scheme. These schemes all put the burden of initial training on the schools in addition to the increased need to induct experienced teachers who move from other areas. In some parts of the country schools also have to induct great numbers of supply teachers.

There was a concerted effort by the DES to create 'fast track' routes to Qualified Teacher Status (QTS) and to attract suitably qualified people who were looking for a change of career or who wished to return to teaching after a career break. Some of the legislation was aimed at teachers who have been trained overseas: in EC countries or even farther afield. This began with the ILEA who recruited staff from Holland, Australia, New Zealand, the USA, Bangladesh, the Caribbean, the Irish Republic and other countries in order to keep their schools afloat. As a preliminary to the open European market in 1992 and as a response to the teaching crisis, the DES relaxed entry criteria for EC trained teachers wishing to work in British schools in 1989 and there has been a significant influx of European teachers as a result.

Circular 13/91 issued in August 1991 provided an even faster track to QTS for overseas trained teachers from non-EC countries and to bilingual instructors who have worked in British schools for at least two years. Schools and LEAs may now apply for QTS on behalf of these colleagues without having to go through the licence period.

The government mounted a campaign to encourage people from other sectors to consider teaching as a career and set up the TASC (Teaching as a Career) group. This follows early initiatives in some local authorities to pursue the same recruitment route. A significant example of this was the Hertfordshire Action on Teacher Supply (HATS) and Mature Entrants Teacher Training Scheme (METTS) run jointly by Hertfordshire and Hatfield Polytechnic, with some input from the petrol company BP. In September 1994, TASC was subsumed into the Teacher Training Agency (TTA).

The Licensed Teacher Scheme

This was defined in Circular 18/89 (DES, 1989a) and allows for unqualified people who meet certain minimal entry criteria (revised in

August 1991 for overseas trained teachers as described above) to be recruited directly to schools by LEAs or by the schools themselves and to teach under licence from the DFE while at the same time receiving their initial teacher training for a period of not less than one term and not longer than two years depending on their entry qualifications. If at the end of this period the teacher is judged to have satisfactorily undertaken the training specified for the period of the licence, s/he is granted QTS.

In the early stages of this scheme some local authorities recruited centrally cohorts of licensed teachers and coordinated their initial training both inside and outside the school, sometimes in partnership with teacher training institutions. Other LEAs have recruited licensed teachers but their training has been entirely restricted to the LEA's own resources or even to those of the school, without recourse to Higher Education (HE). Many schools have actively sought to recruit licensed teachers on their own initiative and to provide a coherent programme of training for them. A final group has been formed where schools have sought to support unqualified instructors on their staffs by applying for a licence on their behalf. It is worth mentioning that all applications for licences have to be authorised by the LEA before they are presented to the DFE. This great variety of licensed teacher schemes have one thing in common: the greater responsibility for their initial and induction training falls on the school and on the mentor, an experienced colleague who is to act as 'critical friend' and guide to the licensed teacher.

All these measures have enabled schools to trawl a very wide pool indeed in order to find teachers and they have been supported by the packages of incentives which many authorities have offered to attract teaching staff, including local pay scales, housing benefits and child-care arrangements. As a result many experienced teachers moved to new authorities, especially but not exclusively in the inner cities, bringing with them a wealth of expertise but also a need to enhance their previous experience with some additional training about inner city issues. Thus schools are now opening their doors to teachers who come from a very wide range of backgrounds indeed, as well as teachers who have received initial training by the conventional PGCE and BEd routes.

A stark example of the magnitude of this challenge can be provided by the recruitment situation in the writer's former school, a large comprehensive in Bethnal Green, East London, in the academic year 1989–90. In September 1989 we welcomed 23 new teachers out of a total complement of about 80 persons. In January we had 10 new colleagues and at Easter a further 4. Of these some were probationary teachers, some were trained overseas (Bangladesh, Australia, New Zealand and Spain), some were supply teachers, some were instructors (unqualified teachers) and some were experienced teachers with incentive allowances who came from other authorities. This picture was duplicated in many other schools in the south-east. No one will underestimate the training challenge presented to the school in its wish to meet the needs of all these colleagues, nor will they be surprised to hear that our success was only partial. The need for schools to concentrate on all stages of teacher training is vividly illustrated by this one case among many.

Retention of teachers: induction training and staff development

To supplement the new recruitment methods employed by LEAs and schools, there have been retention schemes aimed at slowing down the teacher turnover by improving conditions for experienced staff. The glossy brochures which authorities have sent out to prospective candidates for teaching posts, marketing the attractions of working in their respective areas, lay emphasis (among other things) on induction and on-going staff development opportunities.

As has been demonstrated above, once new teachers have completed their initial training they start their careers in British schools with a range of induction needs which is unprecedented in its variety. Programmes for probationary teachers were widely established since the publication of the James Report (DES, 1972) and have involved both individual schools and education authorities, usually working in partnership. Despite the demise of the statutory probation period, there is still a need for these partnerships to remain in place and be strengthened by links with HE.

New teachers with British PGCE or BEd qualifications now seem a relatively homogenous group with induction training needs which can be easily identified. In addition to supporting these colleagues schools must now provide induction and training for staff who may have been trained in any one of the countries listed above, whose own schooling in all probability took place in very different circumstances both at home or abroad, who may have had no teacher training of any description or who may be experienced British teachers with no local knowledge in their new authority.

It is also important not to forget that group of unsung heroes who in many areas have kept schools open in the period of highest teacher turnover, the supply teachers. This often transient group of teachers (which can encompass all the categories described above) has been relied upon to provide continuity for children, often at very short notice. If the role of the supply teacher is not to be reduced to child-minding and pupil achievement is not to suffer, these colleagues should receive induction and training which is at least as comprehensive as that received by trainees and new full-time teachers.

School managers must be acutely aware of the need to provide acceptable working conditions for all teachers through their induction and staff development programmes in a planned and coherent way but they will not underestimate the complexity of the task. An effective whole-school approach to induction and teacher training in all its phases should help schools to retain staff if it aims to address in a practical way some of the difficulties facing teachers taking up a post in circumstances very different to those they have known before. A well planned policy which is shared and understood by all staff will allow the school to face the legislative changes relating to all stages of teacher training as well as the assessment of student, licensed and newly qualified teachers. All aspects and phases of training will then be integrated into staff development and appraisal schemes in a coherent way avoiding the danger of 'bolt-on' additions each time the statutory framework changes. This book seeks to assist schools in the training task both in the text and in the appendices which provide practical guidelines.

Schools which took part in the early school based teacher training schemes, such as the Oxfordshire Internship scheme, were enthusiastic about the positive effects of this approach. Communications within the school and consistency between individual subject areas were improved. Middle managers and subject mentors were helped to cope effectively with staff development for themselves and others and to improve their own teaching and management skills. Staff teaching performance and awareness of pedagogy were enhanced by the climate of discussion about the curriculum and its delivery. Teachers became involved in curricular links with HE, local authority personnel and teachers in other schools. Teacher status and job satisfaction were therefore enhanced and staff felt that this was a real boost to their own career prospects.

This argument was reinforced by the findings of HMI in their inspection of 17 schools with a high turnover in Tower Hamlets and Wandsworth in 1989. Teachers were leaving schools which lacked 'a clear system for school-based support' (DES, 1989d, p 11). Although the report focuses specifically on inner city LEAs, the concept of a well-planned school induction policy is appropriate for all schools in a period when the legislative goal posts are being moved constantly.

Early school-based initial teacher training courses

It was inevitable that the traditional pattern of initial teacher training in Britain which has in this century been dominated by the HE institutions – universities, colleges and polytechnics – would undergo a radical change towards a much greater input from schools. Ministers have been quite explicit about their plans to reform teacher education by shifting the emphasis to schools (Pyke, 1991). The already-quoted DES letter which opened the consultation period on the ending of the statutory school-teacher probation stated 'The secretary of State hopes to announce some firm proposals for making initial training more school based soon.' (DES, 1991f). This was confirmed in the North of England speech of January 1992 and was soon followed by new legislation which is described below.

Theory and practice
Course planning for and the delivery of initial teacher training had hitherto been the monopoly of the HE training institutions. There was not surprisingly a very large theoretical content to these courses. The practical element was embedded in the teaching practice where the student was expected to convert this theoretical background into actual classroom skill in a real school with the help of both lecturers and class teachers. In this arrangement the school has been very much the junior partner. Although many teacher training institutions have long-standing and successful partnerships with receiving schools, these schools have had little or no involvement in course planning or the selection of students. Often the first-line supervisor in the school was not aware of the nature of the course which the student was following back at college. Links between the theoretical input and the school practice could be ad hoc or even non-existent and although the assessment of the student's performance was shared by the school and the training institution, actual decisions about the final pass or fail were often the sole province of the latter which could occasionally lead to surprise and dismay in the school.

There is incontrovertible evidence that students frequently regard the school input as more useful and relevant than the input of the HE institutions. In their survey *The New Teacher in School* (HMI, 1988) HMI found that new teachers felt that their training had put too much emphasis on education studies and too little on the practical aspects of class teaching (p 4). This finding has been borne out in other studies. In a DES evaluation of four school-based PGCE courses, students were found to value most their involvement with schools (Booth *et al.*, 1990, p 88). A joint study by Sheffield University and the Stockholm Institute of Education (Deas *et al.*, 1989) reports students as feeling 'there was "too much theory and not enough techniques"' (p 19).

Practice and theory

The balance of practice and theory began to shift following the James Report (DES, 1972) which accused some courses of being too academic (para. 5, 17). By 1984 when partnerships between schools and training institutions became mandatory (DES Circular 3/84), there were already a significant number of such schemes in existence. In 1989 the DES confirmed and strengthened this development in Circular 24/89 (DES, 1989b) by requiring that local CATE (Council for the Accreditation of Teacher Education) committees should include LEAs and teachers; experienced teachers should be involved in initial training course planning and evaluation as well as student selection, supervision and assessment; they should be invited to contribute to initial training by giving lectures and seminars; all teacher trainers should have recent and relevant teaching experience of not less than one term every five years; all training courses should include 'a sustained period of teaching practice' (at least 75 days); theoretical studies should be closely linked to practical experience in schools; institutions should have a policy statement defining clearly the respective roles of school and HE staff; final award of qualified teacher status is dependent on the completion of successful teaching practice.

New partnerships between schools and training institutions

Prior to the school-based PGCEs which arose from Circular 9/92 (DFE, 1992a) the most significant examples of extended partnerships between schools and HE in initial teacher training were the Articled Teacher Schemes and the partnerships between universities and local authorities for one-year school-based PGCE of which the most publicised has been the Oxfordshire Internship scheme, although there were others, primarily the course based at Sussex University. We describe some schemes below.

The articled teachers' schemes (1990–1994/5)

These were two-year school-based primary or secondary PGCE courses delivered by consortia of local authorities and training institutions. Students in the first cohorts received a bursary of between £5000 and £8000 depending on geographical area and their stage of training. This was considerably more generous than the student grant. Central to the schemes was the role of the mentor, an experienced subject teacher in the school who supervised the articled teacher's training for the entire course. Although the system was seen as an effective way to train teachers, it was short lived because of the high costs involved. The secondary Articled Teachers' scheme ended in July 1994 and the primary scheme in July 1995.

The Oxfordshire Internship scheme
This was a one-year secondary PGCE course and is described fully in Benton (1990). It was seminal in influencing political and academic thinking about school-based initial training. It was characterised by the collaboration of university and local authority schools as equal partners in the teacher training process. It was very well resourced but, despite a reduction in funding towards the end, schools regarded their participation as so important and so useful that their continued involvement was not in doubt. Again the concept of the school mentor was central to the training process, but in this case the mentor worked with the school's professional tutor, a general tutor attached to the school by the university and the curriculum tutor from the department of educational studies at the university.

Left, Right and Centre
In the 1990s some politicians and academics began proposing an even more radical shift in partnership with the schools taking the lead. This has undoubtedly influenced the Conservative government's policy on initial teacher training. On the Right Professor Anthony O'Hear (1991) asked 'whether good teaching may not equally well be acquired while actually teaching in a school under the supervision of experienced practising teachers' since 'teaching is fundamentally a practical ability'. The Labour Party also proposed teacher training schools identified by the LEA and the training institution and which rotate every seven years or so (Straw *et al.*, 1989). Academics have also weighed in: Professor David Hargreaves (1990b), following a proposal by Dame Mary Warnock, advocated teaching schools on the lines of teaching hospitals, with a reduced number of HE training institutions engaged in mentor training, research and in-service training.

A radical pamphlet produced by Professor Hargreaves and other academics from the University of Cambridge Department of Education in 1992 (Beardon, 1992) proposed a system of 'school-led' initial teacher training. Practising teachers in designated training schools would take responsibility for initial teacher training with or without the help of HE. Although differing in some important aspects from government proposals, this pamphlet formed the basis for the subsequent School Centred Initial Teacher Training (SCITT) scheme which is described below (p. 30).

School-based initial teacher training

Subsequent changes to the legislation regulating initial teacher training came thick and fast. Circular 9/92 (DFE, 1992a) provided a framework for the school-based secondary PGCEs which began formally in September 1993. The Circular defined the principles of a 'full' partnership between schools and HE: consortia of schools providing training, a longer period of school practice (60 per cent of the course), the development of competence-based training and assessment, institutional accreditation rather than the previous course accreditation by CATE based on five-year development plans. The arrangements for channelling funds per student via HE to the schools would be left to local negotiation. Quality assurance would be the responsibility of HMI, working with CATE.

These proposals were met with dismay by many HE institutions and with keen interest by many schools, despite fears surrounding resourcing issues (Shaw, 1992b). Although staff in HEIs saw, not without some justification, the Circular as the harbinger of the demise of HE-led initial teacher training, work on the new PGCEs began without delay. Partnerships with local schools were quickly formed despite some early wrangling about resourcing and the 'equality' of the partnership which has never been fully resolved.

Cutting across these local partnerships to some extent is the DFE-sponsored Open University PGCE (Open University, 1994). Since February 1994 this has provided a multi-media distance-learning initial teacher training package for graduates who negotiate their own school-based practice at local schools which provide a mentor in return for a computer provided by the OU. The course lasts for 18 months.

Clearly, therefore, the move to school-based initial teacher training is an irreversible trend, whatever changes of government may or not face us in the future and the onus is on schools to prepare themselves for this new role. There will be many challenges but, as this book shall try to show, the benefits will be legion.

Greater autonomy for schools

Legislation regarding local management of schools (LMS) and opting-out (DES, 1988b) and hints of changes to come regarding the future of LEAs (DFE, 1993a) and teacher training institutions (DFE, 1994b) all demonstrate an increasing interest in making schools autonomous. Standing independent of the local authority and other partners and responsible for its own resources, the school makes the choices needed to allocate those resources in the best interests of pupils and staff. Coupled with the other developments chronicled in this section, this increases the possibility of schools making their own decisions about teacher training in a way which has never happened before.

Local Management of Schools

An increasingly greater part of LEA spending on education is now delegated to schools. Schools and governing bodies are free to make their own decisions about spending via most budget heads. Staffing decisions are left to individual schools as well as decisions about the provision of in-service training, whether in-house or bought in. The freedom to make spending decisions should in theory enable schools to meet priorities with greater flexibility, unimpeded by LEA bureaucracy.

Conversely, schools are seeking increasingly imaginative ways of attracting resources. GEST (Grants for Education, Support and Training) sponsorship, new partnerships with the private sector or other educational providers and lettings of premises are just a few of the ways by which schools are seeking to attract funding or other resources such as people, accommodation or training.

In Chapter 2 the resourcing implications of teacher training for schools is investigated (see 'Resourcing issues', p 67). Suffice it to say at this point that LMS gives schools greater freedom to choose training methods and routes and also puts a greater burden on the institution to plan carefully and to ensure value for money.

Opting-out

As more schools seek and are given Grant Maintained (GM) status and have to provide for themselves those services still retained by the local authorities which continue to mediate their offer to state schools, greater expertise and confidence will be needed in a number of fields, including the induction and training of teachers. GM Schools, like all others, will look for effectiveness, professionalism and value for money, taking on not just the school functions and processes described in this study but those of the LEA as well.

Developing school management
In its report (DES, 1990a) the DES-sponsored School Management Task Force proposes 'a new approach to school management development which focuses attention on the support which should be available in and near to the school and places less emphasis on off-site training' (p 1). Cynics amongst us would see this as a cost-cutting exercise but the intention is clearly in line with the other developments described above, all of which reduce the influence of the LEA and the training institutions and place the decision-making, and hopefully the resources, in schools. The trend for school-based initial teacher training is therefore complemented by a movement to school-based INSET and professional development. It looks as if all teacher training, therefore, will soon be school-based.

Endangered species: the LEA and Teacher Training Institutions
Fears that greater autonomy in a number of processes, including teacher training in all its phases, would be forced on schools were proved to have some substance when the government published the White Paper *Choice and Diversity* (DFE, 1992b) and the blue book, *The Government's Proposals for the Reform of Initial Teacher Training* (DFE, 1993b). These documents laid out the main proposals which would be largely adopted in the 1993 and 1994 Education Acts. In the former (DFE, 1993a) the LEA become only one of the providers of education (along with the Funding Agency for Schools (FAS) and other agencies) where previously it had been the sole provider. LEA influence and power have now been seriously reduced and many still fear that LEAs will eventually disappear.

Similarly, the 1994 Act (DFE, 1994b) was seen as a blow against HE. It established a Teacher Training Agency (TTA) with responsibility for the central funding of all initial teacher training courses in England. It would take over the work of the TASC unit and CATE – both of which were disbanded – and that part of the Higher Education Funding Council's remit which applied to initial teacher training. The agency is responsible for ensuring that the Secretary of State's criteria for training teachers are observed. Among other functions it grants accreditation to providers of initial teacher training which can be either schools or HEIs, provides information about teaching as a career and teacher training and commissions research with a view to improving the standards of teaching and teacher training.

The first chairman of the TTA, Sir Geoffrey Parker, was formerly a headteacher in the independent sector. The chief executive, Anthea Millett, was formerly Her Majesty's Chief Inspector. The Board of the TTA, when announced in October 1994, was felt by some to be largely sympathetic to current government thinking.

School-centred initial teacher training

The 1994 Act also made it possible for the governing body of any school to provide initial teacher training courses to graduates and to join in partnership with other eligible institutions which did not have to be in HE to provide such courses. Schools providing initial teacher training would have to be accredited by the TTA and would receive their funding of about £4000 per student directly from the agency.

The school-centred scheme had been piloted prior to the 1994 Act by selected schools who had been invited to submit outline bids to the DFE in the spring of 1993, to begin training in September 1993 or June 1994. A further group of primary and secondary schools joined the pilot in September 1994, although the majority of schools did not rush to embrace this new opportunity, preferring to work in school-based partnerships. School-centred initial teacher training makes use of schoolteacher mentors as trainers, as do school-based PGCEs. Most have used their funding to buy in the participation of HE, although this is not obligatory.

Therefore, teacher shortages and political will have led to new routes for recruiting teachers which place a greater initial and ongoing training burden than ever before on schools. Concerns about falling standards for pupils and new initial training courses placing a greater emphasis on school experience as well as greater autonomy for schools make a high level of training expertise essential for teachers, as politicians from both sides of the spectrum and academics agree. This new level of teacher expertise will be even more necessary if both LEAs and teacher training institutions cease to exist or have a restricted role in the future.

The following chapters show how schools can prepare themselves to be pro-active and to increase their effectiveness in teacher training at all stages, both in whole-school policies, at the level of the individual and in the classroom. The appendices provide some practical examples of policies and documentation which schools can adopt or adapt to suit their needs for the training function.

Internal factors: the reflective school

The ingredients needed for a successful school-based approach to all phases of teacher training are: whole school communication and reflection on the required systems and philosphy as well as a shared understanding that teacher training does not end with the award of QTS but continues throughout the practitioner's career. This section will also examine the usefulness of teacher profiles in recording this continuum and will show how schools which use initial and ongoing teacher training as a framework for staff development can also benefit from a great improvement in and awareness of management issues and the delivery of the curriculum.

Changing the school culture: whole-school communication

The following information was given to the writer in an interview by a head of department who was asked by her head teacher to be a mentor to two articled teachers: 'When I went to the first meeting I was surprised to find that I was a mentor as I had thought it was an exploratory meeting. I have no time-tabled free time as the time-table had already been written at that stage. I was able to pass on my CPVE work to someone else which was fortuitous. I do not have a lighter teaching load. I get three concessionary periods during which I can be used for cover'. (This mentor also said, 'I think it is a fantastic way to train teachers'.)

Another mentor said: 'Does the whole school take it on? Messages about what it's really about don't get through to all schools and heads'. (This mentor also said, 'I would do another cycle again if the problems were ironed out'.)

Two mentors from another school, both experienced heads of department, had been recruited by their head teacher in the following ways: the first was asked 'Do you want two extra pairs of hands in your department?'; she was given no documentation and had no idea what she was taking on. The other received a letter from his head during the summer holidays, informing him that he was to be a mentor. Despite these early setbacks these mentors appreciated the school-based model of initial teacher training and enjoyed working with other mentors.

Most of the mentors the writer interviewed, despite being enthusiastic about their new role, reported having to negotiate difficult situations within their schools because not all colleagues, even at the highest levels, had a clear perception of that new training role. Similarly, a study of the Oxfordshire Internship scheme which is popular with schools produced the following comment:

> there were other difficulties which arose in connection with certain staff within the school. Whereas mentors had received some kind of training in their role . . . those staff with whom interns were placed to learn about PSE and the tutor role had little knowledge of what they should do, and how Internship had changed the kind of training which interns were to receive in the school (Benton, 1990, pp 98–9).

Such a comment could equally well be applied to any school which receives students on initial training practice or teachers with any kind of training need. The writer, herself a head teacher, carried out an audit of training expertise in her former school (see 'Auditing training expertise' in Chapter 2, p 40) and was horrified at the diversity of practice which this revealed and the blissful ignorance at this lack of consistency in which which she herself had been blithely soldiering on for a number of years. She found confusion over departmental and whole school responsibilities; a lack of clear guidelines; an overwhelming absence of even the simplest induction and training policies in departments; a great diversity in the extent to which heads of department involved students and trainees in school life. Most middle managers felt that they had had no training for this role, although most had learnt from experience. At least two relatively new heads of department indicated that they had done little to contribute to the training of probationers in their teams and did not necessarily see this as their responsibility even though a tick list of suggested activities was provided in the questionnaire.

Teacher trainers are familiar with this problem. The quality of practice in the school is an important criterion in the selection of institutions to receive students on teaching practice. Some training institutions are concerned about the professional role-models and the great range of mentoring quality which they have found. They look for an atmosphere in the school which is conducive to all stages of school-based training in terms of receptive attitudes and willingness to support students and trainees.

Early participants in the secondary Articled Teachers' Scheme found that the success of the school-based training models involved changing the culture of the school. In many cases, heads had not adequately prepared staff for their role in the new courses.

HMI have found similar disparities in school practice when inspecting the HATS scheme (DES, 1990b): 'Support was most successful in those departments which were well-organized and which had carefully designed induction programmes'; and a cohort of European teachers in the London Borough of Havering (DES, 1991b): 'Induction and support in the schools was of very variable quality'.

There is evidence to suggest that a shared whole-school approach not only makes all training far more effective but also encourages other desirable improvements in the school. The deputy head of a community college in Luton which developed its own licensed teacher scheme with a helpful framework for developing basic teacher proficiency (Berrill, 1991) reported that the nature of the school was changed in one year with professional debate occurring between teachers with unprecedented frequency. Similarly, Oxfordshire schools reported a raising of standards. In addition to enjoying the added status of being initial teacher trainers in equal partnership with university lecturers (Benton, 1990, p 101), there have been opportunities for the professional development of teachers (p 108), teacher awareness of educational issues has been raised and pupil learning will be enhanced (p 109).

Steps must be taken, therefore, to change the overall training climate which has prevailed in most schools. It can be summarised thus: decisions about taking students on teaching practice or licensed teachers were made by senior management in consultation with the individual school department involved (or not as the case may be) as a knee-jerk response to need rather than as a result of strategic planning. Little or no training was given to teachers undertaking the role of supervisor. Students and trainees did not experience a consistent school practice. Although some of this practice was very good it was not shared across the school. There is little integration of the training of students and inductees of varying kinds although this would be easy to achieve at least in part. Communication about the various stages of training has been fragmented in all directions: between the training institution and the school, between the schools and other schools, between school management and individual subject teams, between school management and the whole school and between one subject team and the others. There has been no systematic reflection on the criteria for effective teaching. None of these problems is insurmountable and if schools begin to think about training in a structured way the first step towards effective training will have been taken. This book suggests ways in which schools can take the first step and prepare for those that follow and gives some practical suggestions in the appendices.

Recording the training continuum – teaching profiles
A major factor in the fragmentation of our approach to teacher training in schools is that documentation from a teacher's initial training is not carried forward when s/he starts work. Similarly there are no links between the probationary period and the on-going staff development which takes place throughout a teacher's career, except perhaps a file kept in the head teacher's drawer. This erratic approach is unhelpful to the concept of the 'reflective practitioner' which forms the basis of most initial training courses.

One of the most successful innovations of the last decade has been the pupil's record of achievement, a profile which is both formative, in that it enables the student to concentrate on targets for improvement, and summative, in that it is a celebration of individual achievement in a range of aspects. With the guidance of a tutor, the student is therefore able to reflect upon her/his practice using the compilation of the record of achievement as the instrument of reflection and can concentrate on individual action plans from as early as year 7.

There would seem to be undeniable benefits if such a document were available to the teaching profession. It should begin with initial teacher training and be maintained by the teacher throughout her/his career. Most initial training courses aim to help students 'develop both a full range of competences and the ability to analyse and evaluate their own performance.' (DES, 1989b, 6.1.) Teacher trainers in HE are developing profiles to assist the student in this process of critical analysis. The Teacher Training Agency has also consulted on the preparation of a common framework for profiles, using competences, based on preliminary work in 1993 by CATE. The profile could include a summative description of the student's performance against certain known criteria to be used as a basis for continuing training and development in the first teaching post, as well as a record of significant events which took place during the training period such as courses and seminars attended, teaching practice and other relevant items. Such a log would not only benefit the student but also her/his first and subsequent employers.

The CATE model proposed that the profile would contain: The NQT's name; previous educational qualifications and experience relevant to acceptance for initial training; the names of training providers; the course of training (referring to generalist or specialist preparation for primary teaching); the training pattern and locations; subjects studied and age phase for which the NQT has been prepared; a description of any specific projects undertaken and professional interests explored which are thought to be relevant; qualifications gained; date of profile and signatures of authorised representatives of the training provider and of the NQT (CATE, 1994, 3.2). In addition to this contextual information, the profile should include, according to CATE, a descriptive and graded assessment of professional competence and a comment from the NQT (ibid., 3.1).

The profile could later be supplemented with records of the induction period and subsequent stages to make the process of critical analysis continuous and developmental. Another suggestion for the contents of a profile to be maintained by the teacher is:

> a curriculum vitae, a diary of significant events (job changes/promotions etc), a set of short, medium and long term professional development targets of the teacher, notes on INSET together with notes on short and long term effect on the teacher's work, notes on influences on the teacher's work, the shared appraisal document (Hunt, 1990).

Self-evaluation is crucial to the concept of the reflective practitioner. Teacher appraisal enables self-evaluation to take place and provides a framework for recording a teacher's strengths and agreed targets for development. The teaching profile is a suitable instrument for this reflection and can also enable schools to put all phases of the training and development of teachers firmly on the agenda. The profile can either be developed by the LEA in consultation with its schools, by the schools in consultation with HE institutions from which they receive students, or as an exercise by individual schools.

Increasing effectiveness in other school processes

In its study, the School Management Task Force identified several characteristics of effective schools (DES, 1990a, pp 5 and 6). These include:

- leadership;
- delegation;
- purposeful staffing structures;
- clear aims and objectives;
- good communications;
- well qualified, experienced and expert staff;
- high expectations;
- a coherent curriculum;
- a positive ethos;
- a suitable working environment;
- skilful deployment of resources;
- good relationships within the school and the wider community; and
- the capacity to manage change.

The report provides a detailed framework for management development with schools taking the first line responsibility. It recommends that 'At

Figure 1.1 *Generic processes*

Mentor processes each of which can be used in various *School management processes*	
MENTOR PROCESSES	**SCHOOL MANAGEMENT PROCESSES**
assessment of needs	reflection on effective teaching
working collaboratively	team building
interpersonal skills	team leading
focusing on individual training needs	line management
	appraisal
guidance, advice and counselling	training: at all stages
	induction: at all stages
removing constraints	staff development
resolving conflict	monitoring
articulation of subject methodology	evaluation
	guidance for pupils and staff
time management	school review
supervision	development plan
negotiation	curriculum development
observation	improving achievement
assessment of performance	allocating resources
giving and receiving feedback	working with others
target setting	managing change
enabling others to reflect and develop	

school level management development will need to be closely co-ordinated with all other staff development to sustain a unified professional identity'. It is that co-ordination, underpinned by skills required for teacher training that forms the focus of this book.

There are numerous spin-offs for schools which concentrate on the skills and processes required for teacher training. It has already been indicated that in the term 'teacher training' are included the training of students, licensed teachers, newly qualified teachers and all on-going staff development. These skills and processes are common to other school tasks and are therefore described as 'generic'. The generic processes identified, which are central to teacher training, especially using the mentor model, are listed in Figure 1.1.

The other school processes to which these generic processes apply are those which all middle and senior managers and those aspiring to management use in the regular performance of their duties. They should form the backbone of all management training.

In the following chapters there are practical suggestions to help improve local expertise in some of these generic skills and thus promote, as the School Management Task Force suggest: 'better-managed, more effective schools where a confident and competent teaching force can provide a better learning environment for young people' (DES, 1990a, p 14).

Subject content and methodology

The previous section concentrated on generic processes associated with teacher training. These are important and, as has been shown, can be acquired 'on the job' in schools. The other aspect, which teacher trainers fear schools are not so well equipped to deliver, is the transmission of subject pedagogy: content and method. All good teachers work confidently within a framework of subject expertise which they have developed and personalised over the years and which may or may not be wholly up to date. It derives from their own education, initial and ongoing teacher training, local and national curriculum changes and craft developed from their own classroom experience and working with colleagues in their own department and perhaps, but not always, from other schools. Being able to apply this acquired expertise in one's own classroom and being able to pass it on in a developmental way to a trainee without being reduced to 'tips for teachers' are two quite different things. Those who can teach pupils well do not necessarily have the skill to teach adults well.

PGCE and BEd students have traditionally received their education in subject pedagogy from the training institution. The school's contribution has been to provide an opportunity to translate this into classroom practice. The new routes for initial teacher training place a greater emphasis on teaching subject pedagogy on the school. This must be seen as a positive development. To be an effective mentor the teacher must learn to reflect upon the definition of subject content and method and to pass this on to the trainee. Those who are mentors all comment on the enhanced personal development which this process has given them. A focus for reflection on the curriculum, both within the school and working with other providers in universities, colleges and the LEA (as described in the next chapter) is essential and can only serve to improve performance not only for trainee and mentor but also for our pupils. At the end of the day that is what schools are about.

Summary

For the purposes of this book, teacher training is defined as initial training through a variety of traditional and new routes, induction training, ongoing staff development and appraisal.

The rationale behind a concentration on teacher training in schools has been outlined, showing factors which are both internal and external to the institution. The following pages show ways of translating the theory into practice suggesting frameworks which should be easy to develop for any institution. Every school is different and so the reader will not find a neatly finished package for teacher training. The process of establishing a climate for reflection is essential to the change of culture required and it is fully expected that any part of what follows will be the subject of debate in individual schools and either rejected, adopted or amended to suit local circumstances.

Chapter 2 deals with whole school issues which will be particularly interesting to school managers but not entirely irrelevant for middle managers, nor to teacher trainers, inspectors and LEA advisers. Although the focus is on secondary schools, much applies equally to the primary and tertiary phases.

Chapter 3 looks specifically at mentoring and attempts to arrive at a definition of what it is as well as providing ideas for mentor selection and training.

In Chapter 4 specific practical training issues, of particular interest to middle managers, are presented but as in Chapter 2 they will also be of interest to other readers who are planning and co-ordinating training.

Finally, the appendices consist of model policies and instruments for training and induction which can be used as they stand or modified to suit local needs. The bibliography gives a selection of theoretical and practical texts for all those who may be interested in increasing their involvement and expertise in teacher training.

Chapter 2

Whole-school
Management Issues

How good is your school at training teachers?

The first chapter examined the factors which now make it imperative to concentrate on a whole-school approach to school-based (and school-centred) teacher training, which was shown to be a continuous, career-long process. This chapter outlines the steps which need to be taken by school managers who adopt teacher training as a framework for the professional development of their staff. Whole-school awareness is essential to the successful implementation of policy. After analysing strengths and weaknesses of training expertise in the school, managers will need to enhance communication, place teacher training centrally in the institutional development plan, develop and implement clear policies and allocate responsibilities for each aspect of training.

Despite their greater autonomy, schools will have difficulty in shouldering the role of teacher trainers without assistance from other agencies. The second section discusses the possible future role of the LEA, the teacher training institutions and other trainers as well as the possibility of working in partnership with other schools.

Resourcing issues will be uppermost in the mind of most readers and these are pursued in the third section. Finally, the chapter concentrates on accountability and strategies for monitoring and evaluating the school input into teacher training at all stages in the continuum.

Auditing training expertise

Chapter 1 (p 32) referred to an audit taken of training expertise in a

Figure 2.1 *'Developing human potential to assist or individuals to achieve their objectives' (NCVQ Training Lead Body, 1991)*

A. Identify training and development needs.
B. Design training and development strategies and plans.
C. Provide learning opportunities, resources and support.
D. Evaluate the effectiveness of training and development.
E. Support training and development advances and practice.

secondary school and the wide diversity of practice it revealed. This section describes in greater detail how to carry out the audit. Sample questionnaires which can be used are provided in Appendices 1 and 2.

Figure 2.1 shows the National Council for Vocational Qualification (NCVQ) framework for training and development. It identifies five clear steps in constructing training programmes. The first step in any programme of review and development is to establish the current position with its strengths and weaknesses and from there agree targets for change. This identification or assessment of needs is the first stage in designing a training programme and can apply equally to the needs of the organisation as to those of individual trainees.

Carrying out a review of training expertise in a school is sensible whether or not schools intend to extend their involvement in initial teacher training. All schools welcome students and new staff, including newly qualified teachers (NQTs), in most academic years.

In order to identify organisational needs a useful exercise is to carry out an audit of the school as a training establishment by sounding views of both recent and current trainees and those of senior and middle managers responsible for training.

Appendix 1 shows a questionnaire which can be given to trainees and new colleagues in the school. This can include students on teaching practice, licensed teachers, NQTs, colleagues who have had their induction within the last two years and experienced staff new to the school. It asks detailed questions about the induction and training they have received.

Appendix 2 is a similar questionnaire for middle managers asking about the induction and training they have given. When the questionnaires have been filled in and returned it is a simple matter to collate the information given and build up a picture of how training and induction are given and ved within the institution. A summary of the findings should be written up and circulated to all staff. In most schools the picture to emerge will be of a very wide diversity of practice.

This exercise serves several purposes. First, it clearly highlights where improvements can be made in management and organisation and enables this information to be disseminated in an objective way. Second, it identifies good practice and publicises this to a wider audience. Third, senior and middle managers who fill in the questionnaire feel that this process helps them to identify better ways of inducting, training and supporting their teams. Next, it provides a baseline for whole school expectations about induction and training. Finally, it affords the opportunity for the whole school to monitor and evaluate its training practice, taking on board a wide range of views including those of the most junior staff members.

Putting teacher training into the school ethos

Communications

We have seen in Chapter 1 (pp 31–2) how experiences in the first cohort of articled teacher training and the Oxfordshire internship scheme proved that a lack of efficient whole-school communication can impede teacher training processes to some extent. The agenda must therefore be to ensure that *everyone* is informed and not simply those who are directly involved such as mentors, heads of department and senior staff. This section shows how effective communication can become intrinsic using whole-school debate and training, the school development plan, whole-school policies, posts of responsibility and job descriptions.

Careful thought needs to be given to the systematic dissemination of information to all members of ancillary and teaching staff about links with HE, students on teaching practice and other trainees currently in the school as well as the contents of training and induction programmes. This can be done by ensuring that information is given in good time in staff bulletins, on school noticeboards or at staff meetings or staff briefings. Bulletins for parents can also be used to give information to the wider school community. Whole-school policies should be included in the documentation that goes to all members of staff and to governors. Where appropriate they should also be included in the school prospectus for parents.

Where the school participates in new partnerships with HE, the LEA or other schools it is most important that all staff are given clear and detailed information about the scheme and how it differs from previous links so that students and trainees can have a consistent experience in all aspects of their school practice.

Cost-effective planning of training programmes can be best achieved when information about training programmes offered by other providers, such as HE or the LEA, is received in the school in good time to be included in the planning cycle: that is several months before they are due to begin. All too often teacher trainers have contacted schools at the last minute with desperate entreaties to provide facilities for students. Nor was it unheard of for students to present themselves at schools without any prior notice at all.

In the same way, other providers in universities, polytechnics and colleges help to improve efficiency in the schools if they make available to school supervisors the content of the course which students and trainees follow out of school. Equally, college tutors and teachers should be discussing the content of the school experience as well as the taught course. This enables mentors and tutors to link theory and practice in a coherent manner.

Whole-school debate
The need to debate issues relevant to teacher training in whole-staff fora such as staff meetings, team meetings and training days is central to the argument that teacher training in schools can improve performance in a number of different processes. Its importance cannot be underestimated. It is also fundamental as a means of changing the school culture. All debate needs a focus and in the context of this book suitable topics for whole-school consultation may be: the formulation of whole-school policies on induction and training, the criteria for good teaching, the ingredients of a successful induction package, observation and assessment techniques, mentoring, lesson planning, record keeping, subject method and content, performance indicators or staffing structures as well as any of the practical training issues discussed in Chapter 4.

Constructive discussion can take place where a paper on the issue under study is provided in advance as a starting point for debate. The paper can be generated at any level in the school. Some schools which receive students, for instance, have agreed with teacher trainers that the students should carry out special studies on an aspect of school management and organisation as part of their school-based experience and these studies have enabled serious reflection by the whole staff.

The school development plan
This is the major instrument of school planning, involving staffs and governing bodies. The planning cycle begins very early in the year and assists the formulation of policy and the efficient allocation of resources within an agreed structure. Teacher training issues can be considered and addressed within the planning cycle for the school development plan in the same way as all other aspects of school life, as shown in Figure 2.2.

No schemes which are 'bolted-on' without the knowledge, commitment and acceptance of the people who have to make it work will be effective. The simple fact that such issues are being discussed will have the 'backwash' effect of raising awareness, debate and reflection in staffrooms, offices and stockrooms.

Figure 2.2 *Raising awareness about training issues within the development plan*

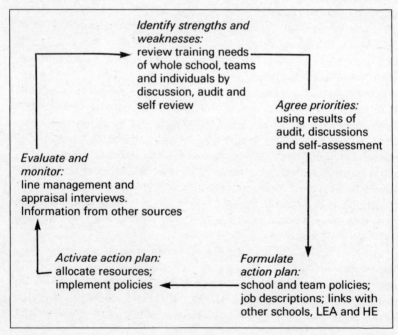

Figure 2.3 *Training issues on which there should be clear policies*

- Initial teacher training: students on teaching practice
  registered teachers
  licensed teachers.
- First appointments: induction, support and assessment.
- The induction of experienced teachers new to the school.
- The induction and staff development of teachers trained overseas.
- The induction and support of supply teachers.
- In-service training for staff from a range of backgrounds and at various levels of seniority.
- Appraisal and line management.

Training policies

Each school will formulate policies to meet its own needs and to ensure consistent expectations and approaches across all teams. Everyone should be aware of what the policies are and their implementation should be monitored by team leaders. Academic and pastoral team policies printed in department and year or house handbooks should reflect whole-school policies and not be separate nor different. Senior managers must make sure that new team leaders are fully acquainted with these as with all whole-school policies.

There can be school and departmental policies on the issues outlined in Figure 2.3. The best whole-school policies are clear and brief so that potential readers are not deterred; an example is given in Appendix 3.

As well as formulating and publishing policies on various aspects of teacher training, schools need to be clear about other related issues such as subject-specific topics; the extent to which training which can be delivered wholly by the school, using directed time, training days, buying in cover etc.; what can be delivered in partnership with other providers; resourcing issues; job descriptions and monitoring and evaluation. Most are discussed elsewhere in this book.

Who is responsible

In any school training at all levels is a collective responsibility which should be shared by all. This is enshrined in the pay and conditions document or teacher's contract which lists training and management duties for all school teachers (see below) and which should be made explicit in relevant job descriptions:

reviewing from time to time his (sic) methods of teaching and programming of work 37.5.1

participating in arrangements for his (sic) further training and professional development as a teacher 37.5.2

contributing to the selection for appointment and professional development of other teachers and non-teaching staff, including the induction and assessment of new and probationary teachers 37.11.1 (DFE, 1994a).

Nevertheless, the first responsibility lies with the head teacher who, with governors, must ensure that appropriate structures are in place, resources are allocated and training regularly monitored and reviewed. They must extend a warm welcome to all new and potential staff and many are careful to conduct the preliminary tour of the school or induction sessions themselves. Additionally, all middle managers share in this responsibility and should be conscious of their duty to enhance their own professional development and that of their teams.

Usually, however, there is a named person who is responsible for in-service training (INSET). This postholder can be called the 'professional tutor', the teacher tutor, the INSET co-ordinator etc. Normally s/he is a senior person on a high allowance or deputy head scale and coordinates all aspects of training and induction including the INSET budget. This often includes links with teacher training institutions. A specimen job description is provided in Appendix 6.

The increasing emphasis on school-based teacher training in all its phases implies that more far-reaching involvement is required embracing a wider staff group including heads of department, other middle managers and subject mentors.

Chapter 3 is devoted to the role of the mentor and its possible variations. This is the first-line supervisor in the school for the student or trainee particularly for subject-specific and classroom matters. S/he is generally an experienced teacher within the same subject discipline whose role is to be the 'critical friend' to the trainee. In the new routes to initial teacher training the role has become somewhat more formalised than that previously adopted by the head of department and in fact the mentor does not have to be the team leader.

Schools will decide to allocate responsibility in ways which best suit local needs. However this is done, clear job descriptions which are known to everyone (perhaps by being included in the staff handbook or in departmental handbooks) make communications clearer, raise expectations, clarify responsibility and form a basis for staff development including disseminating good practice and setting targets in line management and appraisal interviews. The responsibility for training team members should be made explicit in the job description of each head of department or head of year.

This section has highlighted the need to provide a whole-school climate which encourages effective teacher training by carrying out audits of expertise, enhancing whole-school debate and communication, forward planning, developing and implementing relevant policies and allocating specific responsibilities for training at appropriate levels. The following passages look at factors external to the school and the need to work with other partners in order to achieve maximum effectiveness in school-based and school-centred teacher training.

Working with other partners

Despite the new focus on schools as major or sole contributors to the teacher training continuum many think it is difficult for schools to deliver an effective programme of training without some participation by other agencies. The difference lies in the new role of schools as the market controllers, no longer the junior partners. Schools can achieve a great deal more in their role of teacher trainers than has been previously possible and can be pro-active in their choice of partners but there are important aspects which many feel that schools cannot provide. These are discussed below.

Partners or competitors?

Until the Schools Act of 1992, which set up the Office for Standards in Education (Ofsted), the LEA was a major partner for training schools. Now each school is subject to an inspection every four years by inspectors registered by Ofsted and who may or may not be LEA inspectors. This development reflects government suspicion of LEA inspection which was deemed to be too friendly and not sufficiently independent (Hansard, 1991, 300). Ofsted also inspects initial teacher training and reports to the TTA. Other partners for schools are teacher trainers in HE, other schools (singly or in consortia) and independent trainers and consultants.

The radical Right, in the persons of Professor Anthony O'Hear and Baroness Cox (both of whom are members of the first Board of the TTA), as well as others, sees the future of initial training wholly in the schools while the Left has predicted the role of the LEA as quality controller and selector of training schools. As central advisory services in LEAs diminish, this latter role appears increasingly unlikely to survive. Despite greater autonomy for schools and new schemes for school-centred initial teacher training, it is most unlikely and perhaps even undesirable that schools should deliver initial teacher training without any input from other agencies.

For instance, Challney Community College in Luton, one of the first schools to adopt a proactive role in initial teacher training through the licensed teacher route as a precursor to its pioneering involvement in school-centred training, developed a sophisticated method of training both mentors and licensed teachers. Staff found themselves unable to operate it without some outside input and expertise. In the first place, the applications for licences to the then DES had to be endorsed by the LEA. Second, the school bought into EP228, the Open University's original distance learning package for secondary teachers to provide the necessary depth and rigour in theoretical educational studies for its licensed teachers.

There are now radical differences from the traditional collaboration between schools and these providers, not least because schools with delegated budgets to some extent 'call the tune' and local authorities, HE and independent trainers or consultants all compete to provide the training and services that best meet schools' needs. In a certain sense, schools also compete with these other providers for political support, resources and trainees.

Schools involved in teacher training of any sort are in a position to clarify for themselves what they can provide 'in house', what can best be achieved by grouping with other schools and what can be bought in from the LEA, HE or others. In 1990, David Hargreaves, writing before the Schools' Act (1990b) prophetically saw schools being resourced to the tune of about £3000 per student on initial training which would enable them to buy extra staff in addition to the 'necessary expertise from departments and colleges of education as well as from local advisers and inspectors and use information technology and distance learning to ensure adequate depth and breath'. In fact, the first schools to run school-centred training schemes received over £4000 per student to use in this way.

What can schools do on their own and what do they need from other partners?

Secondary PGCE and BEd courses have consisted of the following components: the school practice, educational and professional studies, subject studies and subject method. Before Circular 9/92 the balance between these elements and the degree of theory and practice within and linking each discipline varied from course to course.

In the school-centred schemes, most of these elements are delivered in the school setting although HE input is bought in and some school-centred trainees spend at least one day a week in an HE setting. Teachers in schools are very well placed to deliver the professional craft aspects of initial teacher training, the practical dimension of day-to-day classroom performance which turns students into teachers (and which is not without its own theoretical dimension) and to assess their suitability for the profession. For this reason, teachers trained or partly trained in schools are very employable and need much less induction than those colleagues for whom the bulk of their training took place in an HE institution.

Those who advocate school-based training maintain that schools need help or outside stimulus from advisers or teacher trainers in the theoretical and research aspects of subject method and professional and educational studies. They also need outside support in developing the concept of the 'reflective practitioner'. Teachers perform intuitively and simply do not have the time to devote to the level of educational research and curriculum development which is expected of lecturers. Even the best teachers can be caught in a time warp through sheer overwork, preventing them from reflecting on their craft and moving it forward in a systematic way. In fact, school-based initial teacher training schemes were reported to be meeting difficulties for the 1995–6 cohort as schools dropped out of partnerships with HE due to pressure of work, staff mobility and innovation overload. This made it difficult for HE institutions to find suitable placements for their students. (TES, 1994)

In the best spirit of the new partnerships, school teachers should play an equal role with HE staff in deciding course content and delivery (Shaw, 1992b) and at the same time there should be mutual benefits for both practitioners and theoreticians from the close working contacts they will enjoy and the opportunity to learn from each other's expertise (Shaw, 1995).

The following sections describe the partnerships which schools can explore.

The Local Education Authority

The new role of the LEA as a partner in teacher training can be described in four ways. They are: bankers, quality controllers, brokers of economies of scale and sellers of INSET and support.

In recent years legislative changes have led to a reduction in the central services provided by LEAs as the proportion of the potential schools' budget which can be delegated to schools has increased. LMS and changes in the funding arrangements for local government including rate capping have placed great constraints on LEAs and reduced their influence in a significant way. They are now subject to market forces as schools look to the local authority, as only one of a number of potential providers, for quality and value for money in a whole range of 'products' and services which include the provision of in-service training. This has also led to greater autonomy for individual schools and to speculation about the future dismantling of LEAs.

GM schools are also in a position to buy in local authority services but the remaining functions of the LEA become the responsibility of the head and the governors, for whom much that is said in this section will be relevant. Conversely, as more schools choose to opt-out of LEA control greater spending restrictions will be placed on LEAs and coherent planning will become more difficult.

LEAs as bankers

As long as LEAs survive they are likely to continue to be the channel through which LEA-maintained schools receive the greater part of their funding. The resources which they allocate to schools come mainly from the community or council charge. There are also special funds administered from central government such as the GEST (Grants for Education, Support and Training) budget, the major funding source for INSET and the training of licensed teachers as well as Single Regeneration Budget funding, education support grants and other specially earmarked grants. Indeed we should not underestimate the major part played by government in allocating extra resources (often inadequate) for the implementation of its policies. Logically if central government seeks to relocate teacher training in schools, it should ensure that they are suitably resourced for the task.

To a very great extent, therefore, the level of funding which the individual school receives from local and central government is outside its control. Nevertheless, it is to be hoped that school managers will be consulted by their LEAs about the formula for the general schools budget and for GEST bids and can therefore have some influence on the identification of priorities. Not only must school staffing address the need to allow time for induction and training of new teachers, it must also reflect the necessity to train mentors and provide them with non-contact time to perform their role. In addition there is the question of rewards and incentives for mentors which should be properly provided for in school budgets. LEAs have to decide what is delegated to schools, what is resourced through GEST and other special funds and what is retained at the centre. They can also bid for funding for special projects on behalf of schools.

Quality control

This is achieved through proper funding; inspection, review and advice; monitoring the recruitment and selection of staff; providing guidelines for schools on a variety of issues and being involved in initial training. Initial teacher training providers are also expected to provide self-assessments in addition to inspection by HMI and Ofsted.

Yet it goes without saying that the LEA's role as banker cannot be easily disaggregated from its responsibility for quality control in education, despite the fact that this role is much diminished by the measures in the Schools Act of 1992 to set up Ofsted inspections. New initiatives have a greater chance of success if they are adequately resourced. The LEA has a legal responsibility to ensure that children are receiving the best possible education in its schools and resourcing them properly is primordial. Having said that, it is important to recognise the spending constraints placed on LEAs by central government, forcing them to prioritise.

In addition to well-planned budget allocation, inspection and review of schools (including self-review) is one of a number of means the LEA must employ to assure quality. The constructive and systematic evaluation of schools by LEA and Ofsted inspectors and others should help to identify strengths and weaknesses, enable schools to act upon them and disseminate good practice across the authority. It should lead to an improvement in curriculum delivery, management and organisation which will make schools become better training grounds for prospective teachers.

Advice to institutions and the professional development of teachers should follow naturally from the results of inspection or review with the aim of supporting schools in their quest to do better and to provide a suitable professional experience for everybody, whether in initial training or at later career stages. Where this is done constructively it increases job satisfaction and helps retain staff.

Knowledge gained by LEAs about schools through working with them and through inspection and review plays little part in the selection of training schools. Schools are now autonomous in forming their own partnerships with HE or their own school-centred schemes. Prospective partners looking for good-quality teaching and support, a school ethos conducive to teacher training and suitable subject mentors no longer have a formal source of information within the LEA although this is still thought to be desirable (Earley, 1992). Published Ofsted reports are intended to provide an objective picture of standards and quality in individual schools.

LEA inspectors and advisers can still, if schools wish, exercise a reduced quality-control role at the point of recruitment. Few would be invited to attend governors' interviews for NQTs but they can play an active role in their induction and in the recruitment and training of licensed teachers. Even in this, however, there is great diversity of practice.

As responsibility for recruitment is now one of the duties of the governing body, a very few LEAs continue to operate 'pool' recruitment of first appointments to their schools. The main advantage of this system was the 'economy of scale' in advertising and the quality-control element of the screening processes used by LEAs. The role of the LEA in assuring comparability of standards in training and assessment has now all but disappeared.

Some LEAs have recruited centrally cohorts of licensed teachers and have co-ordinated their training and worked closely with the schools where they have been placed, providing training and incentives for mentors. Again, however, there has been a great diversity of practice. Some schemes are well-planned, employing careful selection criteria and using HE to provide training for both licensed teachers and mentors which will lead to genuine qualifications. These LEAs, such as Hertfordshire and the London Borough of Newham have been determined that the licensed teacher route should not be seen as a second-class path into teaching. Other LEAs have recruited central cohorts but because of the costs involved, training and selection are rather more ad hoc and often do not use any input or expertise from HE. A further group of LEAs have left the recruitment and selection of licensed teachers to individual schools. As the application to the DFE for a licence has to be endorsed by the LEA even if it has been generated by the school, it would be useful if LEAs could provide guidelines for selection criteria and training which could ensure some consistency of practice across the authority.

The two-year school-based PGCE, known as the Articled Teacher Scheme has now been discontinued. Those consortia of LEAs and HE institutions who responded to the DES invitation to bid for pilot schemes in June 1989 found mixed blessings. It is acknowledged that this was an effective way of training teachers, but both HE and LEAs have found the costs involved much higher than anticipated (Abrams, 1991). The Articled Teacher route proved to be an example of positive partnership in initial teacher training where schools, HE and LEAs shared equally the recruitment, selection, training and assessment of students and was seminal in influencing subsequent policy on school-based and school-centred initial teacher education.

Economies of scale

Costs for schools can be reduced by using the LEA as a broker to coordinate the provision of services to a number of schools at a discount. It may still be more attractive for a university or college to work with a cluster of schools through the LEA. In this way, St Luke's College in Exeter has worked through the London Borough of Tower Hamlets to send students on teaching practice to a wide range of schools. In return, the college has provided summer school experience for Year 11 students from Tower Hamlets who may not otherwise contemplate staying on in HE.

Training packages bought from HE can be too costly for individual schools, but are within the reach of LEAs who can maximise GEST funding. To avoid repetition, we shall explore the contribution that HE can make to teacher training in schools at greater length in the following section. While it is perfectly possible for individual schools to work in partnership with universities and colleges, obviously there is even more scope for collaboration where the LEA co-ordinates the links between HE and clusters of schools. This would include the accreditation of professional development.

The best vehicle for this is a teacher training steering committee to act as an umbrella group for planning, communication and co-ordination with equal representation from HE, schools and the teaching profession and some LEA input. Such groups have existed in some areas such as

Oxfordshire and the London Borough of Newham, where partnerships are relatively advanced. Topics for discussion by the group could include course planning, resourcing, selection criteria for training schools, mentor training, monitoring and evaluation and partnership issues.

Most authorities have teachers' centres or professional development centres which, by providing accommodation for meetings and training involving individual schools, clusters of schools and other partnerships, act as the geographical focus. They can also house libraries of professional texts, distance learning packs and training materials which would be too costly for schools to buy individually in any great quantity or range but which are an essential ingredient of professional development and the formation of the 'reflective practitioner'.

Many LEAs still employ induction coordinators who support schools in providing training for NQTs and mentors and by compiling handbooks and guidelines for disseminating good practice in induction and staff development. The LEA in fact retains a legal responsibility to improve coordination between the induction activities of LEAs and those of schools, and receives GEST funding for this (DFE, 1992c).

There is a core of knowledge which all teachers new to an authority need to gain fairly quickly. Induction handbooks and videos can provide essential information about the local area, LEA structures and policies, useful addresses and telephone numbers, maps, national issues and curriculum delivery. It is supportive to find practical information all in one place and can reduce the tension felt by teachers taking up posts in unfamiliar circumstances. Rather than each school 'reinventing the wheel', better quality and greater detail can be achieved if these are produced by the LEA and given to all new recruits whatever their status may be. Either booklet or video format can be used.

The first chapter advanced the idea of a teacher's profile which records key events taking place throughout the professional's initial training and subsequent career and containing documentation which the teacher himself or herself places in the profile. Some LEAs have begun to develop criteria for profiles, linked perhaps with the development of an appraisal scheme, for adoption by all schools in the authority. Usually groups of officers, advisers and teachers from all phases (including those who are newly qualified) would collaborate to produce an appropriate format, which is then produced, distributed and validated by the LEA. This is a useful example of how the wider forum provided by the LEA can yield an end product which has a greater range and credibility than a similar document produced by an individual school.

In the same way LEAs can provide guidelines for schools on aspects of teacher training such as model policies, job descriptions, induction programmes, appraisal schemes, observation pro formas and monitoring systems which ensure a greater consistency of good practice across its schools. Advice on contractual issues to both teachers and governing bodies can still usefully be given by the LEA.

Marketing training

This section concentrates on aspects of training which could be more efficiently offered by LEAs, leaving schools to concentrate on training in classroom practice and assuring some consistency across institutions.

The main ingredients of assistance with teacher training offered by the LEA, bearing in mind economies of scale, should be: induction packages for all new teachers and trainees (several categories are described below), support for the development of competence-based profiles, subject specific advice and training, peer group meetings for trainees and mentors and mentor training. Teacher training, of course is only one of the many aspects of educational practice for which LEAs and others offer training, but our argument is that it provides a useful framework for many of these other aspects.

The Education Reform Act (ERA) and subsequent legislation regarding the delegation of budgets to schools have put the onus on LEAs to offer training of a type and quality which schools will want to buy. Market forces are well and truly at play in this crucial matter of LEA training, with schools at liberty to shop around for training from their own and other LEAs as well as from HE and private consultants. The advantage for schools of buying training from their own LEA, providing it is of an acceptable quality, is that it is offered by colleagues who are familiar with local circumstances and have professional relationships within the schools, often arising from monitoring and evaluation.

Training offered by LEAs on any subject can be varied in its format and can cover all phases of teacher training. Packages for training days across the LEA can be offered, as well as materials and personnel which schools can use for their own local professional training days or for consortia of schools. The training can be school-based, responding to a local need and can be in school time, after hours or it can take place at the teachers' centre and be offered as part of the regular programme. Courses during the school day entail the extra cost to schools of supply cover. Twilight or even weekend sessions are cheaper in that respect but require a time commitment from participants. Similarly, LEA residential centres can be used for training either by the LEA itself or by its individual schools. For such programmes to be cost-effective, LEAs need to consult widely and well in advance with schools in order to be clear about their priorities. These will have been decided locally when schools draw up their development plans.

The publication of the prospectus of courses offered by the LEA as early as possible in the previous academic year also allows schools to consult staff, plan professional development and to budget for course fees as well as supply cover in a systematic way and in accordance with agreed priorities.

It is also helpful when LEAs send details of induction programmes to schools in good time so that schools can avoid duplication.

We have already described how authorities are buying training for licensed teachers and mentors as well as INSET packages from universities and colleges. These would clearly be beyond the reach of most individual schools. LEAs which have recruited licensed and articled teachers centrally have often (but not always) taken responsibility for co-ordinating course planning with schools and invited tenders from HE for induction and/or mentor training. In this way the London Borough of Newham has had partnerships with Christ Church College in Canterbury and the University of East London, while Hertfordshire has worked with the University of Hertfordshire as well as Sussex University. Such packages are expensive to buy and to be successful require not just the initial motivation from the LEA to resource quality training for its staff but also thorough consultation with the staff of participating schools. Where this does not happen, implementation of the programme by schools can be patchy and without 100 per cent commitment. Local management of schools and the increasing delegation of funds to schools has also made such initiatives difficult to sustain, especially where 'buy back' by schools is not guaranteed.

Induction packages offered by LEAs

Induction for NQTs provides an excellent example of co-ordinated LEA provision offering in theory a consistent input of training and information on LEA and national issues. Another advantage is that under such schemes teachers on their first appointments have the opportunity to meet with their peers from other schools and share experiences. Often this is the most valuable aspect of their induction. Many LEAs have been running such schemes for a number of years, in school time, where resourcing allows teachers a reduced timetable in their first year. Now that the probationary period has been abolished there is still a need to train and induct teachers on their first appointments. Resourcing issues and value for money are now even more crucial.

A typical LEA induction programme for secondary NQTs is given in Figure 2.4. This would ideally be complemented by a school induction programme (see Chapter 4) based on local issues as well as subject-specific training, all three aspects being planned in conjunction. The suggested programme may seem brief but consultation with new teachers has revealed a great deal of overlap between LEA induction programmes and initial training courses. New teachers say that the most valuable aspect of induction is the opportunity to meet with their peer group. They find it comforting to discover that everyone is facing the same kind of problems and to share ideas for solving them. Peer group meetings of this kind can be facilitated by LEA advisers or advisory teachers.

Figure 2.4 *An LEA induction programme for new secondary teachers*

This model, presented in a modular framework, could also be used in whole or part for the induction of other categories of trainee.

Welcome session: meet key personnel.
Pay and conditions of service issues including accommodation, child-care facilities and contractual matters.
The structures and facilities of the LEA.
Transport routes within the LEA boundaries.
Teachers and the law.
Visits to other schools and other agencies.
Regular meetings with other NQTs.
Equal access: special needs, race, language and gender.
Subject workshops led by advisers or advisory teachers.
Teachers and the professional associations.
Health and safety issues.
Support services.
Examples of current good practice.
Background materials and research extracts.
LEA policies.
Child Protection.
IT advice.
Regional and national speakers.
Resources for NQTs in the LEA.

Less commonly found, but equally important, are induction packages for new teachers who are not first appointments, especially in those LEAs which have a high teacher turnover. These courses need not be as comprehensive as those offered to NQTs, although some elements could be combined. They could be run in twilight sessions in the autumn term or for a few weeks at the start of each term. A modular structure would make it easier to offer sessions on specific topics to more than one category of teacher, for instance a module on local pay and conditions issues could be offered to both first appointments and experienced teachers new to the authority.

Figure 2.5 indicates some of the topics which could be offered by LEAs as induction for experienced teachers who are new to the area (see also Figure 2.4). Many LEAs also offer mentoring for head teachers new to the authority.

Some authorities, especially in the south-east, are recruiting overseas-trained teachers and running induction sessions for them. Figure 2.6 suggests a framework for an induction programme for these teachers. Because of their different initial training this training should ideally be given before they take up their posts in schools. Particularly valuable would be the opportunity, prior to beginning teaching, to observe lessons and discuss similarities and differences relative to the 'home' system with the peer group, if there is one, and with school mentors. (See also Figures 2.4 and 2.5.)

Some LEAs provide a 'Welcome' booklet for staff new to their schools and this is a sensible and cheaper way to disseminate information which can easily be written down. Similarly, a video format can be used which staff can view at home or at school. Meeting time can then be used for other issues.

Figure 2.5 *LEA induction topics for experienced teachers*

Introduction to LEA personnel.
Core LEA policies.
Child protection procedures.
Training facilities in the LEA.
A survey of LEA institutions.
Off-site agencies and referrals.
Curricular resources in the LEA.
The role of inspectors and advisers.

Figure 2.6 *Induction programme for overseas-trained teachers*

The make up and nature of the local authority.
Key personnel: officers, inspectors and advisors.
The national framework.
Introduction to the National Curriculum.
What to expect in the classroom.
Classroom management.
Assessment and record-keeping.
School policies.
Off-site agencies.
The classroom environment.
Talking to parents.
Pay and conditions.
Teachers and the law.
Equal opportunities.
Support networks.
Taking children out.
Managing discipline.
Useful phrases and jargon.
Professional associations.

Subject-specific advice and training

LEAs can have an extremely important role to play in this aspect of teacher training, which will be difficult for individual school departments to provide effectively because of the lack of time and resources. Schools will very probably be seeking assistance with subject-specific training from outside and HE will be poised to fill the gap if LEAs are not sufficiently prepared.

LEA structures are already in place to facilitate subject-specific advice and training: inspectors, advisers and advisory teachers could focus their support toward teacher training, bearing in mind that this is a continuum which does not end after initial training. For instance, an advisory teacher for a specific curriculum area could act as 'super mentor' or supervisor to subject mentors in schools. Some LEAs, such as Bromley in Kent, did appoint 'super mentors'. Such a person could co-ordinate peer group meetings with subject mentors, update them on recent subject developments, co-ordinate joint discussions and workshops on methodology, resources and curriculum development and generally lend support in the complex business of managing trainees. As with first appointments, mentors value the opportunity to meet with colleagues in the same role as highly as any other aspect of mentoring. Advisers could indeed co-ordinate subject-based training, workshops and peer group meetings for trainees in all categories.

Mentor training

Chapters 3 and 4 discuss the main ingredients of mentor training and argue that there are certain generic skills or processes, additional to subject- and phase-specific skills and knowledge, which all mentors should have in common. We also believe these core processes to be an essential part of management in education: observation skills; working in partnership; recording and report writing; giving feedback; counselling; negotiation and solving conflict; assessing performance and setting targets.

Many LEAs are now offering to their schools mentor training courses combining some or all of these elements. Often they are provided in collaboration with HE and in at least one case are offered in a modular framework three times a year, at the start of terms. Schools can buy into some or all of the modules, as required. Clearly such provision is a good example of LEAs adapting to changing needs and with the growth of different forms of school-based teacher training there should be an excellent market for courses in generic mentoring processes. These should be used in combination with peer group meetings for mentors as described above and could include input on the management and organisation of induction, examples of good practice guidance on observation and review meetings (Earley, 1992 p 4).

Working with HE institutions

Schools can form new partnerships with HE in several ways, some of which compete with or have replaced services offered by LEAs. Schools can work with HE as 'training schools' in school-based PGCEs, the concept first mooted in this country by Mary Warnock and David Hargreaves; by using distance learning packages for teacher training developed by HE; by buying INSET and school improvement packages from HE and by negotiating accreditation for professional activities as part of modular qualifications.

Training schools

David Hargreaves (1990a) set the cat among the pigeons when he suggested radical reforms of initial teacher training. A great polemic ensued with academics and teacher trainers weighing in as well as politicians from the Left and Right. The idea of training schools, akin to the teaching hospital model, was first mooted by Mary Warnock. In the article mentioned and later ones also in the TES, Professor Hargreaves put forward the rationale for placing initial training in schools. He referred to a growth in confidence and skill among schoolteachers in all aspects of training and professional development and a growing demand for school-based INSET. The devolution of budgets to schools and school teacher appraisal are leading to better planning. In their survey *The New Teacher in School* (HMI, 1988) HMI had commented on the discontinuity between initial training and induction and the dissatisfaction felt by new teachers at the lack of preparation afforded in training courses in certain topics which could easily be addressed in schools. These topics included: teaching less-able pupils, classroom control and administrative and pastoral duties. In a later article, Professor Hargreaves (1990b) went on to suggest diverting resources currently spent on student teachers to provide advanced training for experienced teachers. If schools were to receive a sum per student (he suggested £3000) they could reward staff and buy in expertise from HE and LEAs. Information technology and distance learning could be used to provide sufficient depth and breadth. This would free HE staff to carry out necessary research and development with experienced schoolteachers. Since the publication of these articles there has been an inexorable shift towards training schools, as described in the first chapter.

It is of course a question of degree. Schools have always been involved in teacher training and there seems to be an inescapable logic in the argument that training should happen in the workplace rather than in the ivory tower. Providing practical examples and role models and ensuring continuity between all stages of teacher training seems sensible. HE staff are naturally threatened and defensive about the shift in emphasis. They argue that not all teachers feel capable of taking on the main responsibility for students. This is of course true, and this book suggests a model for rectifying this gap, but it is also true that not all HE staff are completely up-to-date in school management and procedures despite the relatively recent requirement that they spend a proportion of their time in schools (DES, 1989b).

To the writer, the optimum solution does not lie in schools 'going it alone'. It has already been shown how schools need external stimulus in articulating subject methodology and general education studies. Teacher training would be very flat if it were reduced to on-the-job apprenticeship without the extra dimension provided by colleagues who are able to engage in research and to have an overview of a variety of institutions. Partnerships between schools and HE, where the larger part of the training takes place in the schools or the local area and where school staff have the benefit of training by and collaboration with HE staff should be advantageous not only to teachers and lecturers but also to students. The Oxfordshire scheme is usually held up as the seminal influence but there have been other schemes involving a larger school-based component such as the one run by the University of Sussex and the Articled Teacher Schemes. In 1989 HMI reported on the partnership between Trent Polytechnic and Nottinghamshire LEA, whereby 12 polytechnic tutors were placed in schools annually (DES, 1989h). A senior teacher was seconded by the LEA to act as secretary to the joint local committee for initial training and to co-ordinate the scheme. Teachers were released from classroom duties by the tutors and were to use the time to support the new colleague and to carry out curriculum development. School-based PGCE courses are now in place all over the country and schools have become partners with universities and colleges either by invitation or through their own initiative. The extent of partnership can be decided locally but evidence shows that HE still tends to take the lead.

The very real benefits to both school and HE of these partnerships are legion. The basic framework for school-based initial training is a link between a teacher training institution in HE and a particular school or cluster of schools in a specific area. The school contracts to host a number of students from the HE institution for a larger proportion of the training course than has been possible with the system of block or serial teaching practices up to now. Although the training is accredited by the college or university, the bulk of it is actually carried out in the area local to the school by school staff (the mentor concept) who have planned the course and been trained by HE staff. Schools receive funding for this work from the HE institution although this implies economies have to be made elsewhere. Additionally a 'barter' system can operate incorporating some or all of the elements listed below.

Above all, these partnerships enable HE institutions to meet the Secretary of State's criteria which now require a greater emphasis on the participation of schools in initial training. All institutions offering PGCE and BEd courses now have to be accredited by the Teacher Training Agency. In addition, there should be better communication about course content between all parties and clearer role definition between school and college tutors.

Schools benefit from recruitment possibilities from a cohort of students in whose training they have participated and who need relatively little induction. School staff can have access to HE facilities such as libraries which can otherwise be costly to join. In some cases accreditation packages have been negotiated to validate teachers' work and professional development as part of modular diploma or degree courses. This attractive incentive is discussed below.

Students feel their training is relevant and that they are genuine members of the school community. There is greater consistency in their school experience as expertise accumulates in the training schools. They are given practical experience of many of the issues which the Secretary of State now requires to be included in training courses such as information technology, pastoral and administrative responsibilities, child protection procedures, home-school links, multicultural understanding, working with children with special educational needs, links with the world of work, the legal framework of education and team work. Where teaching profiles have been developed they can be carried through with no break in continuity to the first teaching appointment.

College tutors are able to carry out their 'recent and relevant' teaching practice (DES, 1984, 1989b) in schools with which they have productive links. Where this occurs it provides a valuable extra resource for schools in time, expertise and curriculum development. College staff can also help with the planning and presentation of school-based or LEA INSET. They could also act as 'super mentors' or consultants on specific issues. They can train teachers to assess classroom performance and act as catalysts for other forms of professional development. Finally, they have less time-consuming travelling to do between schools which are geographically far removed from each other in order to visit a handful of students not very regularly.

Distance learning packages
HE can also be involved with schools by marketing distance learning packages to be used in school-based and school-centred teacher training. The best known and most widely used was the Open University's EP228 'Frameworks for Teaching'. This was a general education package designed in blocks to enable qualified graduates to join part-time courses

leading to QTS. It was taken through an institution which runs PGCE courses, of which it would form a part. It was not subject-specific and parts could also be used in induction programmes. The blocks were: Introductions; Working with Pupils; Working in Classrooms; Working in Schools; Schools, Teaching and the Wider World. Each block was broken down into components which looked at specific issues relating to statutory criteria. The course material included readers, collaborative projects and audio-visual packs. Assessment combined continuous assessment and a final examination, each equally weighted. Students were allocated a course tutor who may have worked at the HE institution and were expected to be members of self-help groups. EP228 has now been superseded by the Open University Distance PGCE described in Chapter 1.

Another distance learning package for initial teacher training has been developed by South Bank University, Manchester University and West-minster College, Oxford. Although originally aimed at the independent sector the course team hope that maintained schools would also find it useful. The course, 'Distance Education for Teaching' was intended to form one part of a one-year PGCE or 'one year of professional training on a concurrent undergraduate course (3 year BEd or equivalent), building on 2 years of higher education'. It could also be used for training instructors or licensed teachers. The early structure was: school experience and teaching practice on the job as an employed teacher; residential periods equalling 45 days; distance learning materials equalling three-eighths of the course or 180 hours. The school experience should cover knowledge of more than one school, observation of other teachers, teaching subjects other than the individual's own specialism, be supervised by a school mentor and an HE tutor and should be spread throughout the course in a carefully structured way.

There are other distance learning packs which deal with specific subject topics such as the STEP scheme – Science Teachers Education Project – details of which are given in the bibliography (STEP, 1974a and b).

Understanding British Industry (UBI) also market a useful programme called, 'Teachers' Business' aimed at enhancing trainee teachers' knowledge and understanding of preparation for the world of work. (UBI, 1993)

It is therefore perfectly possible for schools to plan their own initial training courses, especially for licensed teachers, using any of these materials which are currently available on the market.

Packages for in-service training

Many HE institutions are already well into the business of selling INSET packages to LEAs, schools and individual teachers. This includes mentor training packages. There is also a growing market for school improvement packages such as the Cambridge Institute of Education's IQEA (Improving the Quality of Education for All) scheme (Hopkins and Ainscow, 1993). There is a potential here for competition between LEA INSET providers and HE, especially as the former's future appears to be in doubt. HE can fulfil exactly the same role as that outlined for LEAs earlier in this chapter (see p 54). With fully delegated budgets schools can choose value for money and quality.

Clearly HE institutions are as well-placed as LEAs to offer the whole range of professional development and INSET and if initial training does move into schools this will free HE staff to work more creatively with experienced schoolteachers, as predicted by David Hargreaves (1990a, 1990b).

Accreditation

Not all HE institutions offer modular degree or diploma courses but this is becoming increasingly common. In addition, many institutions accredit prior learning by which teachers' own work can count towards a degree or diploma. For instance, school teacher mentors working with the then Thames Polytechnic were offered the incentive of 40 units towards an MA, for which the total number of units required is 120. Mentors value this incentive even more highly than financial remuneration as they feel it lends status to their work. The idea of accreditation of teachers' professional activities and INSET in this way could be easily extended by negotiation between schools and universities or polytechnics. In other cases licensed teachers have been offered accreditation to diploma or even PGCE level when they have attended training courses organised jointly by LEAs and HE. This avoids the label sometimes attached to the licensed teacher route that it is a 'cheap and nasty' way to train teachers with an inferior level of quality assurance when compared to PGCE or BEd routes.

Working with other schools

In many ways consortia or clusters of schools are better placed than individual schools to deliver all stages of teacher training. The clusters can include schools from all phases from nursery to tertiary.

Apart from the advantages of geographical proximity there are other benefits relating to economies of scale: training for mentors, trainees and new teachers can be purchased jointly at a saving to all schools involved; peer group meetings and workshops in subject-specific areas can easily be arranged; a cross-phase cluster of schools working with one HE institution will offer a diversity of experience which is now considered very good practice in initial teacher training; expertise and good practice can easily be shared. With the growing uncertainty over the future of LEAs it makes good sense for schools to form links in this way.

The more formalised clusters of schools are those operating the school-centred initial teacher training schemes and the schools working in clusters around CTCs to train technology and science teachers with the Smallpeice Foundation and Roehampton Institute (CTC trust and DFE, 1994, p 7).

Working with independent consultants and trainers

The growing army of private consultants in education and management whose glossy brochures land daily on our desks can of course offer all the services described above which are currently offered by LEAs and HE. Most consultants have wide experience in education and management and can tailor packages to suit the requirements of individual schools or groups of schools.

Since legislation has changed the structure of school inspection and advisory services as well as seriously reducing the influence of LEAs, schools are obliged to look to private consultants as well as to HE for training and support.

This section has described how schools will need to work with other partners when delivering teacher training and has shown views on how autonomous schools can be in delivering teacher training. There are some aspects which many feel that schools cannot offer to a satisfactory level of depth and quality without outside help. At present resourcing and quality control for maintained schools is channelled through LEAs. There are still advantages for individual schools or clusters of schools to work with and through LEAs, not least of which is the benefit of economies of scale.

The competition between LEAs, HE and private consultants has generated a wide variety of training packages for a growing diversity of purposes. These include personnel, materials and training which can act as a catalyst for subject-specific and general education studies; distance learning packages to facilitate school-based training at all levels; accreditation of teachers' work; mentor training; induction and the use of library and training facilities. The power to choose now lies with the schools and therein lies the major shift in emphasis.

Resourcing issues

Schools with delegated budgets have to look very closely at the spending and income-generation implications of all their activities so that money is spent wisely in accordance with the development plan and in the best interest of pupils and staff. This section identifies what income training schools can expect, what they will need to pay for and suggests alternative ways of resourcing, some of which have been touched upon in previous sections.

All schools already have a staff development programme and many manage their own INSET budget so there is an element in this section of teaching one's grandmother to suck eggs. Nevertheless it is useful to examine the resourcing of training as a whole because it is seen as a career-long continuum. School managers will already have deployed many of the resources needed for teacher training, and hopefully it will be apparent that being a 'training school' should not incur unnecessary expense. On the contrary, money and other resources spent on teacher training will be to the direct benefit of pupils.

Income for school-based and school-centred initial teacher training

Most income for training teachers in schools is brokered by the LEA in the form of the delegated budget and GEST funding for various activities either devolved to schools or 'top-sliced' to fund central activities or staffing. Grant-maintained schools receive funding for training through special grants.

For receiving students on school-based PGCEs, schools receive a proportion of the funding that HEI has received, initially from the HEFC and latterly via the TTA. The proportion of the total sum (approximately £4000 per student) that schools can expect is determined by local negotiation and in 1995 averages £1100. There is a widely held belief in schools that this amount is insufficient and should be fixed by legislation rather than by local bargaining. Many practitioners in schools would also appreciate greater clarity about how the remaining £3000 is spent by the universities. There can also be problems when a late shortfall in students allocated to a school leads to budget deficits after the reduced timetable for mentors is written. Delegated budgets can only be used to pay for the education of pupils, not students on teaching practice. For each student on a school-centred initial training programme the entire sum per student is paid directly to the validating institution – that is, the school – who can use it according to their own priorities.

The Training and Enterprise Councils (TECs) are increasingly becoming a rich source of funding for teacher training, especially for projects such as Investors In People, Total Quality Management and vocational training, although again arrangements are defined locally.

What do you need to pay for and how can you do it?

School managers in training schools need to budget for personnel, time, training courses, materials and accommodation. Budgeting on this scale requires careful planning, well in advance and inclusion in the school development plan. Sources of 'income' include not only the school's own deployment of staff, supply cover, incentive allowances, rooms and directed time but also links with other partners (see previous sections) and

Figure 2.7 *Items which training schools have to resource*

A. Personnel	Source
Professional tutor: body vacancy and allowance	Staffing budget
Mentors	Already on staff
Rewards for mentors	Incentive allowances or LEA GEST budget and/or accreditation
Supply cover	Staffing or INSET budget
Admin support	Staffing budget, TTA funds.
Consultancy	GEST
B. Time	
For induction	Staffing or INSET budgets; may need to be at start of each term

For mentors to carry out role	GEST, TTA funds or use HE staff
For observation	As above or use non-contact time or HE staff
For interviews between staff (debriefing/appraisal)	As above or use directed time
For mentor and trainee training	Use HE staff, directed time, INSET budget, training days, TTA funds
For peer group meetings	Use directed time, training days

C. Training courses

Mentor training	LEA GEST budget, school INSET, discount through links with other schools, free by HE staff in return for teaching practice, private sponsors, LEA advisory staff, TTA funds
Induction	LEA GEST budget, links with other schools or HE as above
Distance learning packages	As above
Staff development: group and individual	As above if part of same framework; little extra cost
New Headteacher training	Headlamp from the TTA

D. Materials

Books, training packages, etc.	At no cost if provided by LEA or HE through libraries otherwise GEST or TTA funds

E. Accommodation

For meetings and training	School accommodation, LEA teaching centres, LEA residential centres, HE seminars and training rooms, links with industry

through those links items which can be obtained through 'barter', free of charge or at a discount.

Figure 2.7 sets out items which have to be 'paid for' and the most likely sources of funding.

Monitoring and evaluation

Schools should have formal structures for evaluating the success of their training policies at all levels. The process of self-review is essential to school development. How this can be done is described in the following paragraphs.

Accountability

Each team leader from the head teacher down is responsible for the training, support and supervision of his/her team. This responsibility should be specified in job descriptions. Even though senior staff such as the teacher tutor may have specific responsibilities for the management of INSET, middle managers must be aware of their responsibilities toward all categories of trainees in their teams and must be pro-active in implementing school policies.

Line management meetings

Many schools already operate a system of this sort which goes some way along the path to formal appraisal, but does not necessarily involve lesson observation. The use of a formal and regular structure for a two way dialogue is welcomed by staff. The benefits of line management are:

- Communication is enhanced
- Teachers in small departments feel less isolated
- Teachers feel supported
- Feedback can be given in a non-threatening way
- Time for reflection is welcomed
- Needs are identified
- Confidentiality is observed
- Good practice is disseminated
- School policies are monitored
- Targets are set
- Can be used for induction
- Can be used for counselling/negotiation
- Consistency is enhanced

Team leaders and their line managers can easily build discussion on training issues for students, licensed teachers, new colleagues, etc. into this agenda to ensure that expectations are being consistently met. Minutes should be kept of the meeting and the audience for this written record is negotiated between the two partners. Line management is a sort of half-way house between mentoring and appraisal and skills needed for successful line management are among the skills identified as core or generic mentoring skills. An agenda for line management meetings is suggested in Appendix 8.

Appraisal meetings

The system of line management described above forms a strong basis for an appraisal system which would monitor the same issues in a rather more formal way. The essential elements of an appraisal system are:

- Pre-interview meeting
- Self-appraisal
- Lesson observation
- Collection of information from other sources
- Appraisal interview
- Written statement including agreed targets
- Follow-up
- Review meeting

There are clear links between line management, appraisal and mentoring and the same core skills are needed for each process. Appraisal for schoolteachers tends to be developmental rather than supervisory.

Self-review

This applies both to the school and the teams within it as an essential part of the school development planning cycle as well as to the individuals working in the school at all levels. There can be no development without reflection on practice. Teachers find that regular formal structures as described above – planning for school development, audits of school training needs, line management and appraisal – do afford an opportunity for reflection and for enhancing one's professional performance. Institutions can therefore allow individuals and teams an opportunity to review their own progress regularly, as part of the planning cycle. School managers should regularly review the effect of teaching by trainees on pupil outcomes and the financial viability of school-based and school-centred training.

Performance indicators

These are formal indicators which schools can use to assess their own progress. They are not meant to be used in league tables for comparison with other schools. Measures of the success of training policies could include:

- Comments in evaluations of training and induction by trainees
- Whether training issues are addressed in departmental handbooks
- Use of the school for teacher training by HE institutions
- Staff turnover
- Recruitment of teachers from their 'own' students
- Numbers of staff willing to be mentors
- Numbers of mentors taking up accreditation/further study
- Numbers of mentors being promoted
- Improvement in pupil outcomes: test results
                                   examination results
                                   behaviour
                                   attendance.

This section has shown ways in which school managers can evaluate the success of their training policies and has described indicators which can be used when reporting to staff, governors, parents and working partners in the training process.

Summary

This chapter has concentrated on whole-school issues which managers must consider when planning teacher training either as part of the conventional staff development programme or as a full blown 'training school'. These management issues are: identifying where the expertise is, school ethos and communication, development planning, whole-school policies and the allocation of responsibilities. Schools can work with a number of other partners, principally in LEAs, HE, other schools and from private consultancies. Resourcing and monitoring and evaluation are practical issues which all school managers address daily.

The next chapter looks at issues which, although presented in a whole-school framework, are of particular relevance to middle managers. It begins by examining the role and function of the mentor. Chapter 4 looks at practical training topics.

Chapter 3

Mentoring

Trying to arrive at a definition

This chapter examines in detail the role of the mentor in schools. The concept of the school teacher mentor is still relatively new and academics and practitioners alike are struggling to find a common definition. The chapter begins by showing the wide variety of interpretations of mentoring which exist in education and other fields. It then shows how mentoring requires skills which inform other important management processes in schools and demonstrates a range of ways in which mentors can work with other partners. The benefits and challenges for mentors and their schools are outlined. Criteria for the selection of mentors and for their training are suggested. A model job description for a subject mentor is given in Appendix 7. This should assist school managers in the selection and training of candidates for this important role. A growing list of publications on mentoring is reflected in the bibliography for those who wish to do further reading.

What is a mentor?

There are as many variants of the function 'mentor' as there are schemes which use them or partners with whom they work. Here are just a few samples:

'Trainers and developers' (National Council for Vocational Qualifications).

In teaching:

Supporting a colleague professionally who is less experienced than the mentor (London Borough of Newham, undated.)

A supervisor oversees. A mentor guides and teaches. These roles often overlap (Wilkin, 1990)

The mentor has a major role in the support and assessment of the articled teacher in the classroom (Roehampton Articled Teacher Consortium, 1991a).

The curriculum tutor and the mentor are together concerned with the professional development of articled teachers in relation to classroom practice. . . . The mentor enters into a voluntary partnership with the curriculum tutor and with the other mentors in that subject. S/he contributes the experience of an established teacher and the perspectives rooted in that experience. . . (University of Oxford, undated).

. . . a mentor teacher with expertise in the specialist subject of the intending secondary teacher . . . (DES, 1989a).

The mentor will be a practising subject specialist within the subject dept. of the GAT's school. The mentor will be an experienced teacher of the subject . . . (Thames Polytechnic, 1990b).

In order to provide effective support and a framework of professional development the mentors will need to develop training and supervision skills including: . . . coaching, peer teaching, guidance and counselling, assessment of classroom practice (Thames Polytechnic, 1990b).

Experienced but not very senior . . . someone committed to good teaching and professional development (HMI, 1988).

In other countries:

'Pedagogic counsellor': French teacher training system (DES, 1989c).

Mentors in the USA are also variously known as 'school supervisor', 'cooperating teacher', 'role model' and 'coach' (DES, 1989g).

. . . teachers of demonstrated ability and expertise. . . . The mentor's primary responsibility is to guide and assist new teachers (Feiman Nemser *et al.*, 1990 on the mentor teacher program in California.

In adult, community and further education mentoring has been routinely used in the training of teachers and other professionals for some time:

Mentors should generally be experienced practitioners who are considered able to offer appropriate advice and support to participants in the scheme. All mentors will be required to attend a specific course of training. . . . A mentor's role is not to direct a participant's activities but rather to enable a participant to work in a self-directed way, by acting as a 'sounding board' for ideas, a source of information about training opportunities and a professional support throughout the process of accreditation. . . . The mentor's role is not as a trainer but a guide and assessor of competence achieved . . . (Adult Literacy and Basic Skills Unit, 1988).

In health visiting and social work:

Support and assessment of trainees is divided between field-work teachers, health visitor managers and lecturers. In social work there is also a training team consisting of the college tutor, the study supervisor and the line manager.

Subject mentors

This term can be used to describe the head of department, line manager or any experienced colleague who assumes responsibility for some aspect of the school-based training of new teachers. This is not a new nor revolutionary departure as the best team leaders have always been conscious of the need to promote the development of members of their team, especially newcomers. With the advent of teacher training courses with a much higher school-based content and which have re-examined the balance between theory and practice, the term 'mentor' has acquired new significance. Ideally, in a secondary school, it should be someone who is not the teacher tutor although s/he should oversee the work of subject mentors. It is unlikely that one person could effectively take responsibility for the day-to-day support of all the categories of trainees whether they be licensed teachers or first appointments. As the central issue should be the performance of the teacher in the classroom, directly affecting pupil achievement, in most cases individuals or pairs of trainees should have a subject mentor from their own department. (This may not be necessary for experienced teachers who come from 'out-county'.)

Phase mentors

Some trainers believe there should be both a subject mentor and a 'phase mentor', that is someone who could be responsible for guiding and inducting the trainee in general educational matters relating to the school, the LEA and the national framework, leaving issues of classroom practice to the subject mentor. As such induction will often be parallel for students, newly appointed teachers, licensed teachers and others, this role could be assumed by the professional tutor. Clear forward planning should enable this person to utilise induction programmes both in the LEA and in the school simultaneously for first appointments and other categories.

Mentors for new heads and deputies

Mentoring as a training and induction method is now considered so important that in autumn 1991 the DES announced funding of about £2m to provide mentors for newly appointed heads and deputies. The process of mentoring at this level seems to require the development of an understanding of the school; clarification of the new role and job; providing feedback on performance; highlighting opportunities for greater effectiveness and giving personal support (Kelly *et al.*, 1991). These functions clearly overlap with the subject mentor role.

Super mentors and generic mentoring

The training of mentors is expensive and time-consuming. For the first cohort of articled teachers mentor training was undertaken in a variety of different forms, usually by the HE institution in partnership with the school and/or the LEA. It has become clear that whoever underwrites mentor training in the future, be it schools, LEAs or training institutions, not only will there need to be more thought and structure put into training but also it will not be practical for training to be delivered every year to a new cohort of school-based mentors (usually one mentor for each pair of students).

The skills required for mentoring are highly specialised and in some schemes have been on a par with the skills which teacher trainers develop over many years' experience. It would be difficult to deploy a system whereby a large new group of teachers was trained to be mentors in expensive courses run by HE in every academic year. Schools could simply not afford the cost of the training nor the supply cover.

Yet, as will be shown, there is a core of these skills which, if deployed consistently in our schools, could assist in training and development throughout every stage in a teacher's career, including the support and supervision of staff and pupils as well as appraisal and to which every manager should have access. This is the concept of generic mentoring. It seems clear that a concentration on these skills as a primordial ingredient in the training of teachers as managers would lead to a greater emphasis on the reflective consideration of methodology by individual teachers in our schools. This would in turn lead to higher pupil achievement. It would be more cost-effective for institutions to buy into a super mentor, a person trained in mentoring who could assist, guide and advise subject mentors in schools as well as facilitating meetings and workshops between mentors from different schools. Although the role could be undertaken by the professional tutor there are other ways of achieving this aim.

For instance, advisory teachers could be trained easily for this role, which is akin to their current role in most LEAs. Such a person could either

Figure 3.1 *Mentoring as part of school processes*

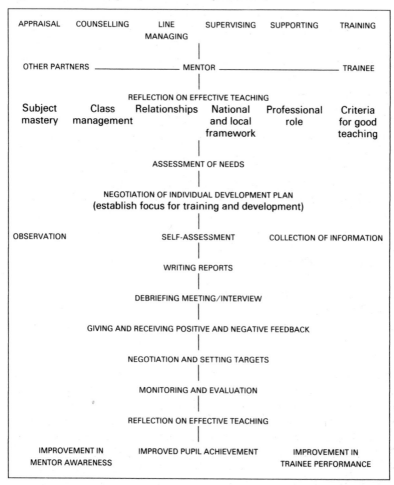

be funded by the LEA or clusters of schools could buy into a super mentor/advisory teacher. For new heads and deputies an existing or recently retired senior school manager would be an appropriate choice. GEST priorities include the induction of all categories of teachers and so the INSET budget could be used if schools could not deploy a portion of their staffing budget for this purpose.

Mentoring within other school processes

Schools which adopt teacher training as a whole-school policy will have the benefit of integrating mentoring and supervision within a range of fundamental school processes. This is best demonstrated in tabular form as seen in Figure 3.1.

Mentors and other partners

Figure 3.2 shows the different partnerships in which mentors or supervisors may be involved for various categories of trainee. It can be seen that school-based mentors have more support from other agencies in initial training schemes and arrangements for the induction and assessment of NQTs, but that for other categories of trainee, in particular the experienced teacher who comes from out-county or who returns after a career break, the mentor or first-line supervisor carries the entire burden of induction and support. The mentor, therefore, has a different role in each case because of the variety of partnerships.

A more standardised approach to these partnerships and clear communication inside and outside school could close some of the gaps seen in Figure 3.2. These partnerships can be a catalyst for the generation of new ideas in the school but there can also be problems as we shall see below.

The rationale for mentoring

This section looks at the benefits of mentoring for individual teachers and schools and at some of the problems that have surfaced in the early stages of school-based schemes so that planners and managers can be clear about organisational factors which are needed to ensure the success of mentoring.

Figure 3.2 *The role of the mentor and other partners*

Mentor works with	HE: universities, polytechnics and colleges	LEA: inspectors, advisors and advisory teachers	School management	Department management where HOD is not the mentor
Student on teaching practice	•		•	•
Registered teacher	•		•	•
Licensed teacher	?	?	•	•
NQT		•	•	•
Supply teacher		?	?	?
Overseas-trained teacher/instructor	?	?	•	•
Out-county teacher			?	?
Returner		?	?	?
Headteacher	•	•	•	
Staff development	•	•	•	?
Other trainers and consultants also offer staff development training				

? indicates that partnerships exist in some schemes but not all.
• indicates that partnerships exist.

The benefits for teachers

'In terms of professional development it's the very best thing that has happened to them', said an Oxfordshire head teacher on the teachers who are mentors to interns in his school.

Various incentives are offered to teachers who agree to be mentors. In some schemes (by no means the majority) an incentive allowance is given or a temporary honorarium equivalent to an allowance. More often mentors go unpaid but most agree that there are rewards associated with mentoring which have nothing to do with money. The professional associations may not agree and there has been some debate about the ethics of asking teachers to take on these duties without payment.

In the time-honoured tradition of the teaching profession, where practitioners are not rewarded by higher pay, there can be slightly less tangible but equally important rewards such as being given the extra free time to do the job. In Chapter 2 it was shown how mentors need time for training, meeting with the trainee, observation and debriefing; increased non-contact time is therefore a valuable incentive. Mentors see it as even more important than payment.

They also value highly the improved career prospects afforded by the role (mentoring looks good on a curriculum vitae or testimonial) and the opportunities for accreditation of their work in school as part of further study. They feel that their status is enhanced and they like being identified as good practitioners and to share good practice. They appreciate having the chance to discuss pedagogy with others and to attend peer group meetings. Those who work in small departments feel that their isolation is lessened.

Mentors attest that they are learning skills which are transferable to their other professional activities such as counselling and negotiation and they enjoy learning fresh ideas from their contact with trainee teachers.

Conversations with mentors from a wide range of schemes revealed that they appreciated the opportunity to reflect on their own practice. Although conscious of the often onerous duties they had taken on, which they clearly articulated, all were enthusiastic about mentoring as an opportunity both for self-development and teacher training.

Benefits for schools

This constitutes the main thesis of this book. Some of the benefits for schools of mentoring have been described in earlier chapters: raising awareness about effective classroom practice; providing a climate for discussion about teaching methods and subject content; the enhancement of a variety of school processes all of which lead to an improved classroom experience for pupils with an ensuing rise in achievement.

Schools can also expect to retain capable people by expanding their rewards and opportunities and by offering better job satisfaction for staff. As well as the opportunities for mentors, trainee teachers have expressed high motivation and improved performance from mentoring. Routes which lead to more effective young teachers will of course benefit schools.

Problems associated with mentoring

All, however, is not rosy. There have been real problems experienced by the first formal cohorts of mentors, mainly to do with time management, training and unclear communications.

Mentors have heavy burdens of both management and mentoring duties. One mentor reported to the writer: 'College tutors can escape but mentors are there all the time'. Senior managers and other teachers are not always aware of the difficulties involved and are not always able to resource the non-contact time which is essential to effective mentoring. Mentors often find they are used for cover when they are about to sit down with their trainee or to observe a lesson and sometimes have to prioritise between equally important duties of, say, a head of department and mentor.

Some mentor training has not always been systematic and relevant and this book represents an attempt to enable school managers and others to get that right. Sometimes communications between the providers – LEA, HE and the school – are not clear and timely and mentors are confused by conflicting demands on them and not clear about what they or their trainee/s are supposed to do or what deadlines have to be met. They may not receive full and detailed information about course content or dates of meetings to be held outside the school. All these factors put extra pressure on already over-burdened teachers.

In schools where there is not a whole-school approach other colleagues do not always share the same perceptions about the training role, as described in the first chapter, and this can lead to conflicts for mentor or trainee which the mentor has to resolve.

Weak or difficult trainees make heavy demands on the mentors; equally, not all those selected to be mentors have the correct interpersonal skills. Again this can lead to conflict and unhappiness. Finally, mentors report that it is hard to reconcile the role of friend with that of assessor. Not only do mentors have to guide and coach the trainee but in initial training schemes they are also responsible for 'pass' and 'fail'. This burden can be lessened when responsibilities are clearly defined in a supportive way between all partners. The quote which opened this section shows the difference between the college tutor who can 'escape' and the mentor who is there day in and day out with the trainee. Problems which do arise are therefore exacerbated.

Mentor selection

Having looked at the benefits and pitfalls related to mentoring it is clear that selecting the right person to fill this role is extremely important.

The purpose of the job

The varied definitions given at the start of this chapter help us to be specific about what mentors actually have to do and are encapsulated in the job description in Appendix 7. Essentially, they provide professional support to students and new teachers in their department in the development of classroom and subject skills. This is the most important aspect of the job, when the experienced teacher is expected to pass on the 'tricks of the trade' to the novice.

Mentors work in a paid or voluntary capacity with other partners both inside and outside the school but in the final analysis the mentor is expected to have the overview of the trainee/s in question and to relate the theory learnt in studies to the practice witnessed and enjoyed in the classroom and the school. They combine the functions of coach, guide, counsellor and adviser as well as being a source of information to the trainee about subject content, methodology, training issues and school procedures. Advice has to be constructive and to go beyond simple criticism. Mentors have to make sure the trainee knows about schemes of work, school policies, other colleagues, the needs of pupils in a range of age groups and abilities as well as the lay-out and resources available in the school.

The mentor is expected to remove constraints which hinder the trainee in fully benefiting from the training programme. These can include school accommodation factors, lack of access to resources and difficulties experienced with pupils or colleagues. At times sensitive negotiations have to take place.

As well as friend, the mentor can be the assessor. S/he has to assess the trainee's needs at the start of the programme and continue to ensure that they are met by constructing a training package which can include a teaching programme, lesson preparation, knowledge of the pastoral and administrative life of the school, a calendar of meetings, observations and visits. S/he is also responsible for or involved in interim and final assessments of written material and teaching practice, depending on the category of trainee. Above all the mentor has to enable the trainee to reflect upon and develop his or her own performance.

Who is suitable to be a mentor?

Again, the skills, experience and knowledge required are summarised in the job description given in Appendix 7.

In secondary schools mentors need to be subject specialists with some successful teaching experience under their belt, although they do not need to be the head of department. They should ideally be well read and take an interest in updating their own subject knowledge. Not only should they be familiar with a range of teaching methods and resources and be known to use them successfully but they should be able to pass on that knowledge to others in a way that empowers them as teachers. This latter skill is not automatic to all teachers! Good mentors will be able to work collaboratively with the trainee, the partners in HE and the LEA and with other colleagues in school.

An essential prerequisite to effective mentoring is good interpersonal skills. Mentors should be encouraging, empathetic, good listeners, reflective and analytical, well organised, flexible and approachable. These qualities enable the trainee and others to relate to the mentor and lend the mentor credibility in the training role. The mentor must be able to help the trainee to identify good practice in classroom teaching and adapt it successfully for him or herself.

Mentor training

Why train mentors and what should the training consist of?

Having now identified suitable persons to be mentors, schools and their partners must ensure that effective training is given for this very demanding and central role.

Schools which use teacher training as a focus for their staff development or who seek to become training schools in partnership with HE or otherwise will have to ensure that there is consistent good practice across the whole school. Training in mentor skills for middle managers therefore becomes essential.

Teacher effectiveness and pupil achievement will not be enhanced without including a broad debate on classroom methods, effective teaching and subject pedagogy in the school development plan.

Teacher training is a complex process involving skills which the ordinary classroom teacher may possess but which may not be highly developed. These individual skills are listed briefly here and discussed at greater length in Chapter 4. The main ingredients of mentor training would be in subject methodology and its articulation, general pedagogy as well as the core or generic mentoring processes of needs assessment, counselling, negotiation and conflict solving, observation, assessment of effective teaching, report writing, giving and receiving positive and negative feedback, setting targets and working collaboratively.

Who should train the mentors?

The advantages of economies of scale to be derived from working in partnership with the LEA, HE or clusters of other schools have already been described. Despite the apparent 'Do it Yourself' focus of this book it is undeniable that the best and most cost-effective mentor training will be provided outside the school by trainers experienced in these issues and as described in the 'Resourcing' section of Chapter 2. Some LEAs have had the foresight to provide mentor training, as in Newham where core skills training has been provided centrally at the start of each term.

Much of this training is being done by teacher trainers from universities, colleges and polytechnics but it could be done equally well by LEA advisers or by management consultants. There is also speculation that commercial and industrial trainers will enter the arena.

In the end, though, it will be up to school managers to ensure that their mentors are enabled to do their jobs by having proper training. The current move is toward school-based staff development. For those school managers at senior or middle level who wish to improve performance in their schools there are ways that training can be done 'in-house'. The following chapter and the appendices offer some practical suggestions.

Chapter 4

Practical Training Issues

Setting the context: why should teacher training be an issue for middle managers?

Having set out in the earlier sections of this book the reasons why schools are now becoming closely involved in school-based and school centred teacher training, and having looked at wider whole-school issues of policy, management and organisation and examined the role of the mentor, we now come to practical issues for middle and senior managers which can be addressed in a whole-school training programme. We begin by looking at National Council for Vocational Qualification (NCVQ) standards for training and development.

Moving to the local arena, the benefits of whole-school debate on effective teaching and collaborative working are summarised. We look at various ways of assessing effective teaching. After discussing induction to the school or the department we consider the core or generic mentoring skills. Practical instruments, including policies, check-lists and job descriptions, which schools can adapt for their own use are provided in the appendices.

A national framework for training and development

It is interesting that while the lead bodies of the NCVQ are seeking to establish competences and national standards for all occupations up to the equivalent of post-graduate level, primary and secondary school teaching still seem unlikely to be part of the move toward vocational qualifications (Jackson, 1991). This does seem strange at a time when teacher training at all levels is becoming school-based and school centred, because NVQs are essentially about the assessment of performance, according to agreed criteria, in the work place or a simulation of the work place. The reasoning behind this apparent anomaly is that there is already a body which measures initial teacher training against pre-set criteria, and that body has been CATE and is now the Teacher Training Agency working with Ofsted. Presumably school teacher appraisal will 'take care of' the assessment of performance at later stages in a school teacher's career, but it seems a shame that members of other professions can aspire to accreditation of their day-to-day professional activities as they move onwards and upwards but teachers are denied this opportunity unless they are prepared to take on the further extra study needed for additional qualifications. It could be argued that this devalues the daily work of classroom teaching and running a department or a year.

The question of using competences to assess performance is left until later in this chapter, but the question of the NCVQ is introduced at this point because while the NCVQ has not been able to establish a lead body for school teaching, it has been able to produce national standards both for management and for training and development. It is worthwhile looking at the latter briefly. While this may appear to be a digression, it seems important to address the question of validating the work of middle and senior managers in school when they are increasingly being asked to take on board teacher training and staff development in the work place. Currently there are no direct routes to validating the work of school-based initial teacher trainers and assessors, although a growing number of teachers are acquiring TDLB 32, 33 and 34 qualifications to assist them in the assessment of GNVQ courses.

The five main steps to 'developing human potential to assist organisations and individuals to achieve their potential' defined by the Training and Development Lead Body (TDLB) were given in Figure 2.1 (see p 41) and are a good example of the commonsense approach to competences which the lead bodies have so far deployed. In the introduction to its standards the TDLB also illustrates six main categories for which standards can be used, in addition to the design of qualifications. These categories are of interest to school middle and senior managers who are seeking a coherent framework for teacher training at all career stages. They can also be applied to the use of criteria or broad domains to articulate effective teaching; this topic will be returned to later. In the lead body document the six categories are broken down into detailed component criteria.

Although there are no current plans to apply standards to school teacher education it is worth noting that NVQs are already available to teachers in some sectors and being piloted in others. Among the bodies working with TDLB on the units for assessment and verification published by NCVQ in March 1991 were City and Guilds of London Institute (CGLI), BTEC and

Figure 4.1 *Use and application of standards*

JOB DESCRIPTION

- as a basis for formulating job descriptions
- to provide a common reference for responsibilities within the training and development function

RECRUITMENT AND SELECTION

- to provide a comprehensive source of descriptions for the abilities needed by candidates
- as a measure to compare candidates objectively
- to determine which candidate best fits the demands of the post

TRAINING

- to establish clear objectives for the training of trainers
- to shape the development of new training materials
- to measure the effectiveness of existing training materials

STAFF DEVELOPMENT

- to measure progress by individuals
- to establish priorities for further development

APPRAISAL AND ASSESSMENT INCLUDING SELF-ASSESSMENT

- as a basis for appraisals of performance
- as a focus for discussion of individuals' strengths and weaknesses
- as a guide for individuals to monitor their own performance

ORGANISATIONAL REVIEW

- to evaluate and review the training strategies and policies with (sic) the organisation
- as a source of ideas for new policies on training.

Above all the standards can be used to inspire change and improve the effectiveness of training and development. It is important that these wider applications should not be overlooked (NCVQ TDLB, 1991, p 4).

the Royal Society of Arts Examinations Board (RSA). CGLI offer a course 7307 for training teachers in further and adult education and the RSA offers qualifications for teachers and trainers in a range of fields including management and information technology.

If such standards were applied to school teaching they would not only provide a national framework for school-based initial training (particularly for licensed teachers who do not at present enjoy the benefits of any such framework) but also a structure for progression throughout a teachers' career which indicated the range of skills required for each management level.

In the absence of any national standard, examples of what the author considers to be good practice in school-based teacher training are provided in the following sections.

The whole-school debate

Chapter 1 discussed how all school managers should achieve a whole-school culture which enables reflection on teaching skills, effective induction and training to take place. Team leaders are responsible for the local implementation of whole-school policies and their translation into practice at classroom level where the real work and purpose of the school occurs.

Middle managers will certainly need to be aware of the whole-school management issues outlined in Chapter 2, especially those in schools which have a high turnover of staff or who receive large numbers of students or licensed teachers. To assist in the implementation of school policies at the 'chalk face' this section aims to provide a practical framework for middle managers to raise their own awareness and that of their staff about training issues. It will be clear that consideration of the issues presented in this section will provide a helpful basis for integrating many of the initiatives on which we are currently embarking: not only those to do specifically with training and induction but also new curriculum and assessment arrangements and appraisal.

Many of the suggestions in this section will be familiar and may already be part of your practice. Team leaders may very well have more effective solutions already in place to some of the questions raised. The aim is not to provide neatly packaged answers to some very difficult questions such as 'What makes an effective teacher?', or 'What does every teacher need to know?'. The fact is that there is not one single answer to these questions.

Although there is a central core of knowledge and skills which we shall attempt to define, each institution and each subject department or year team will identify a range of different knowledge and skills which its teachers must acquire to be fully effective. The reflection and debate which should take place within teams to identify effective teaching knowledge and skills and the resulting conclusions are as important as any other training method. In their 1987 survey (HMI, 1988, p 10) HMI stated that those responsible for training and induction need to understand that more attention should be paid to defining the levels of competence in different professional skills which may be expected at the conclusion of training. Schools where this reflection and debate have taken place report an increased job satisfaction for staff, both trainees and supervisors, who feel that their own performance is improved. This must in turn lead to the primordial outcome for schools: improved achievement for pupils.

This debate can take place either on school training days on, for instance, 'Helping a Trainee' which could combine whole-school input with departmental time, or can be used as part of team training in department or year meetings. To start the discussion it may prove useful to look at the summary of domains for teaching competence given in Appendix 10. This has been put together from a number of documents where attempts have been made to define what all successful teachers should know. The sources include DES circulars on initial teacher training, the probationary period and licensed teachers; appraisal pilot projects; HMI surveys and reports; documentation from teacher training institutions in HE; individual schools and literature on classroom skills. The list given in Appendix 10 is only intended to be the starting point for discussion. Schools can add and subtract their own domains according to local consensus.

Once the domains which suit a particular school have been decided, they become the basis of a coherent framework for a whole range of training and management processes hopefully applied consistently across the board: needs assessment, setting expectations for staff, lesson observation, support and supervision, assessment of student, licensed and first appointment teachers as well as for appraisal.

The next step is to break each domain down into its component criteria; this process is dealt with in the section which follows.

Check-lists and competences

Who uses them already?

In the current race to define effective teaching and to construct a framework which ensures consistency of training and practice, various agencies have attempted to articulate criteria for good teaching. These include: the DFE (circulars relating to licensed teachers and initial teacher training as well as the teacher's contract); the now defunct Council for the Accreditation of Teacher Education (CATE); teacher training institutions, some in partnership with receiving schools (eg, Oxfordshire Internship scheme's List of Important Abilities which are reproduced in Appendix 9), University of Cambridge Department of Education, Christ Church College in Canterbury with Newham schools, St Lukes in Exeter; LEAs (Hertfordshire Licensed Teacher Scheme); HMI (two surveys on the 'New Teacher in School', report on training teachers for inner city schools), the DFE, the TTA and individual schools (Challney College). We have described how training and assessment by competences are used in National Vocational Qualifications and have alluded to the CGLI 7307 course for teachers in further and adult education. They are also used to train and assess teachers of adult literacy (The Certificate in Teaching Basic Communication Skills).

The use of competences to describe and assess effective teaching has been in use in other countries for some time. Check-lists of criteria have of course been in use for many years in the United States, sometimes to extremes, and examples can be found in the Florida Programme and in the Boyer Topics, teaching competences devised by a committee chaired by ex-secretary of state Boyer, which are used in the Provisional Teacher Program in New Jersey. This programme and a central or regional definition of what every new teacher should know and be able to do in operation in France have been reported on by HMI (DES, 1989c, 1989g). Scottish teacher training institutions have used a competence-based check-list for some time.

Various pilot schemes for teacher appraisal, the ACAS report of June 1986 and the report of the National Steering Group on the school teacher appraisal pilot study in 1989 (DES, 1989e) have also identified teacher competences which are listed in prompt sheets for the self-appraisal stage.

The DFE also expects competences to be used in the induction of NQTs (DFE, 1992c).

Ticking boxes or broad outlines? Defining the content

As we have seen, the procedure begins by defining broad areas of competence or domains (see Appendices 9 and 10) which cover the range of skills that teachers need to teach effectively. There is no standardised format for these lists of domains which in existing examples range from 5 broad areas to 20 or more. The most open-ended profile simply gives the broad headings while the most minutely detailed checklist will break down each domain into its component competences or criteria, as in the American systems. The most extreme of these contains 1276 criteria which are ticked when they are judged to have been achieved. In *Classroom Teaching Skills*, Ted Wragg (1984a) refers to the dilemma facing those who construct such lists:

> Some skills are very complicated. There is a debate whether the act of teaching should be seen as a whole or is capable of being separated into discrete if interrelated skills.

Once the school has decided on the broad formula and listed its areas or domains it must examine how each domain can be observed and measured by individual teacher actions and by pupil behaviour and outcomes. Appendix 11 is an example from the Oxfordshire list of important abilities of how domains can be broken down into measurable and observable criteria. In this case the domain is 'Classroom interaction', described in the list by 12 pupil outcomes. In a document produced by history mentors and tutors each pupil outcome is further disaggregated into teacher behaviour. Noticeably the two elements of pupil and teacher actions are kept separate but shown to be interrelated.

Whole-school debate on criteria for effective teaching will concentrate on general teaching skills, but secondary schools also need to consider criteria which are specific to the different subjects covered in the curriculum. The question of subject-specific criteria which directly influence what happens in the classroom have hardly been addressed in any scheme, most of which concentrate on generic teaching skills. It seems realistic to assume that the best forum for considering subject-specific criteria and enhancing knowledge and delivery includes not only the school practitioner/s in their department teams but also representatives from other schools and subject 'experts' from the LEA and/or HE, as shown in Chapter 2.

TEACHER TRAINING IN SECONDARY SCHOOLS

Progression

Not all schemes involving criteria or lists of competences address the issue of progression, ie, the different expectations one would have of teaching skills during the first teaching practice, compared to that of a teacher on his or her first appointment, or a head of department or even a head teacher. This would be an important issue for debate in schools. How do you describe and assess these skills at different levels? Attempts to define a progression follow. They vary from fairly crude lists such as the teaching contract given in pay and conditions documents to rather more sophisticated attempts as in the Exeter University project.

The conditions of service for teachers, otherwise known as the teachers' contract, include reference to some functions which can be expected of managers as well as defining the contractual duties for all teachers. However, these are not listed in any coherent order which would imply a progression. Random mention is made of:

> contributing to the selection for appointment and professional development of other teachers and non-teaching staff, including the induction and assessment of new and probationary teachers (37.11.1);
> co-ordinating and managing the work of other teachers (37.11.2);
> participation in administrative and organizational tasks . . . including the management or supervision of persons providing support for the teachers in the school and the ordering and allocation of equipment and materials (37.12.1) (DFE, 1994a).

In general the teachers' contract expects all teachers to undertake all duties and makes no distinction for seniority so a clear indication of skills and duties required at different career stages will not be found there.

Let us then consider the documentation relating to school teacher appraisal. The prompt sheets for the appraisal of teachers included in the report by the National Steering Group using the document produced by ACAS (DES, 1989e) differentiate between standards which newly qualified teachers could be expected to achieve and those which a main grade teacher could aim for. Interestingly the prompt sheet for new teachers is more detailed than that for main grade colleagues and concentrates more heavily on teaching skills.

Thus, appraisal schemes tend to concentrate on articulating higher level skills at each career stage: differentiation by outcome. A further method is to use grades. Some schemes, such as the one used in the ILEA (Tower

Hamlets, 1991b) and subsequently in at least one Inner London Borough, for the assessment of newly qualified teachers used a grading system:

Grade 1 – for teachers who have not yet reached the standard required for the satisfactory completion of probation.
Grade 2 – for teachers who are well on the way to achieving the satisfactory standard above.
Grade 3 – for teachers who need to make marked improvements in order to achieve the satisfactory standard above.
Grade 4 – for teachers whose performance is giving rise to serious concern as to whether they will be able to reach the satisfactory standard above.

An argument against using grades rests on the unreliability of subjective assessments. One assessor could give a quite different grade from another. One way of counter-balancing this effect is to make the criteria for assessment as detailed as possible so that judgement is based on factual evidence and not subjective opinion.

Other schemes have identified progression by the use of descriptive statements for each level. In the Tower Hamlets/Thames Polytechnic articled teachers' scheme (Thames Polytechnic, 1990b) the levels jointly devised by the mentors were as follows:

Level 1 – Not yet evident.
Level 2 – Basic awareness.
Level 3 – Growing competence.
Level 4 – Basic proficiency.
Level 5 – Extended proficiency.

The disadvantage of this scheme is that no criteria are given by which the mentor, assessor or supervisor can objectively place the trainee at a specific level. Assessment is left to a subjective intervention and further, trainees would have no clear expectation of what they were expected to achieve to attain each level of performance.

The system used by St Lukes College in Exeter (Kirkman, 1990) for their primary PGCE is unique in that it identifies nine dimensions: ethos, direct instruction, management of materials, guided practice, structured conversation, monitoring, management of order, planning and preparation and written evaluation for which specific criteria are articulated at eight levels. Students are expected to reach level 5 by their final teaching practice. Experienced teachers would aspire to level 8. Students, school staff and teacher trainers have found the clear guidance offered by this system both helpful and developmental.

To summarise, the question of progression does not necessarily have to be addressed through grades or levels. There is a core of essential teaching skills which all practitioners must display in order to teach effectively (eg, ensuring the safety of children in the classroom, laboratory or workshop; ensuring that the majority of pupils are on task for the majority of the time). It would be an interesting exercise for staff teams to identify what they consider to be the essential skills without which no teacher can be considered competent. Apart from these core skills there are other criteria which define good teaching which effective teachers would be expected to achieve most of the time. The fact is that teaching is an organic and flexible science which cannot be reduced to a mechanistic check-list. A teacher can be a very good teacher and still not achieve a tick in every single box. We all have off-days in which the normally well-disciplined beginnings and ends to our lessons are less than perfect. The question of progression can therefore be addressed by identifying which teaching skills need attention and focusing on them until we feel that particular target has been met. A new focus for development is then agreed. The question of target-setting as a developmental tool is addressed below.

How are check-lists currently used and how can this be improved?

Figure 4.2 shows how the different check-lists or sets of competences that are mentioned in this book are used for different purposes in different schemes. It attempts to show which schemes use broad areas and which use detailed check-lists. Teachers wishing to concentrate in greater detail on check-lists or domains of teaching competence will then have some idea of where to look for inspiration. It should be clear from the diagram that no correlations are currently made between the different types and functions of check-lists which teachers encounter at different stages in their careers. Consistency of expectation and delivery would be improved if this were the case. The same criteria used to describe and assess teaching skills at initial training should be carried through the first appointment to career-long appraisal.

An exception to this lack of standardisation in assessing teaching competence was the project at Challney Community College in Luton: 'A Foundation for Excellence' (Berrill, 1990). This scheme was devised to meet the needs of licensed teachers employed by the school. The scheme

Figure 4.2 *Some examples of how check-lists describing teaching skills are used*

INITIAL TRAINING	NQTs	SELF-APPRAISAL/ ASSESSMENT
Diagnostic/summative	Diagnostic/summative	Summative/diagnostic
DOMAINS		
Licensed teacher criteria	LEA assessment schemes School based assessment schemes.	References Open testimonials
Oxford model Exeter model Most HE institutions		
CHECK-LIST		
CATE criteria Challney model USA model NCVQ model City & Guilds 7307 Adult literacy model	HMI blueprint as described in 'The New Teacher in School' surveys, 1983 and 1987	School observation schedules Prompt sheets in appraisal studies
Current applications		
PGCE, BEd students, licensed and registered teachers	Not commonly used for other purposes	Sometimes used for peer group or other focused observation
Possible applications		

Setting expectations for supply teachers, overseas-trained teachers, teachers new to the school and returners from a career break. Also for job descriptions, needs analysis, developmental training and school review including observation and assessment, including self-assessment and appraisal.

integrated competence areas associated with effective teaching, giving feedback based on these areas (the formative process), the teacher/mentor relationship, observation, induction and teaching profile as well as review and target setting. The development of such an integrated approach for schools and their partners is to be recommended.

Some HE institutions and LEAs have sought to build a composite picture of the national framework for effective teaching by extracting the criteria given in DES circulars for use in initial training by CATE (DES, 1989b) and combining them with the criteria articulated in circular 18/89 (DES, 1989a) which is about licensed teachers. This process yields a lengthy and cumbersome document which does not make a clear distinction between what things teachers should be able to do (skills) and what things they should know (knowledge). A further attempt to clarify what is essentially a muddied picture was made by the National Curriculum Council (NCC) in its document: *The National Curriculum and the Initial Training of Student, Articled and Licensed Teachers* (NCC, 1991) This booklet attempted to define the curricular skills, knowledge and understanding which teachers should develop 'as a part of their wider professional training'. School teacher mentors and supervisors will find it informative as a starting point.

What else can we use check-lists for?

Once a school has waded through the documentation listed above or alternatively referred to Appendix 10 of this book which summarises all the broad areas listed, and has decided on its criteria or competences for effective teaching, the same list can be used to provide a unified and consistent approach for many school processes as shown in Figure 4.2. This is neatly summarised in the NCVQ rationale seen in Figure 4.1. Checklists can be used for:

Clarifying expectations about teaching performance to: students, licensed teachers, first appointment teachers, teachers from overseas, returners, supply teachers, other new but experienced teachers, mentors, new and experienced heads of department.

Needs assessment in order to devise a training programme: students, licensed teachers, first appointment teachers, teachers from overseas, returners, mentors and any other category deemed appropriate according to local needs.

Observation: students, licensed teachers, first appointment teachers, peer group, for appraisal, for open reports and references, by senior management, head of department or mentor.

Assessment including self-assessment and school review: by all practitioners.

Appraisal: by all practitioners.

Setting targets: by all practitioners.

This section has taken a lengthy look at the main instrument which schools can use to inform teacher training at all stages: the description of effective teaching. It has been shown how it can consist of either broad headings related to classroom performances (domains) or detailed criteria by which performance can be seen to be effective or not (check-lists). A few examples have been given of how others have attempted to define effective teaching and it has been shown that there is no clear or standardised format. There is a particular gap where the definition of subject-specific teaching skills is concerned. Schools must decide if they are to address the issue of progression and how they will do so. Finally, having constructed their definitions, schools can use them in a diagnostic, formative or summative way to structure all processes to do with management, development and assessment of teaching skills.

The following section deals with another topic central to effective teacher training: induction.

Induction

Chapter 2 looked at the LEA's contribution to induction on broad issues of local and national significance and the opportunity it affords to meet staff in the same position. This section discusses the importance of induction both to the school and to the department or team as the first stage in any staff development or training. Suggestions are made for types of documentation to give to the new colleague and the Appendices give a model check-list for facilitating induction to the school as well as suggestions for school and department induction. Not all new colleagues arrive with the same training and experience and so examples are provided of modules which can be adapted to different categories of new teacher. Induction is needed for student, articled and licensed teachers as well as first appointments (NQTs), supply staff and other experienced but new staff however senior they may be.

Giving a warm welcome

First impressions count and the quality of the welcome given to new and potential staff can be a crucial factor in their recruitment and retention. In their report *Training Teachers for Inner City Schools* (DES, 1991c) HMI report that student teachers have described the friendliness of many inner city schools, especially in London, as a critical element affecting their decision to teach there. This would apply undeniably to all schools.

It is important that the student, the candidate or the new teacher, even if highly experienced, feels genuinely welcomed to the school. This means that time has to be laid aside to conduct a preliminary visit as part of induction to a school. The check-list given in Appendix 4 indicates important aspects of school organisation and of the induction programme which should be included in the preliminary visit. Appendix 5 shows how the list can be modified for different categories of new staff or trainees. If the person being inducted is given a copy of the check-list it enables him or her to be aware of what he or she needs to learn in this first stage of contact with the school.

Many head teachers enjoy personally welcoming new staff and giving them a tour of the school and this is very good practice. While it is essential for newcomers to meet the head, the initial contact and tours of the school and the subject area can be organised by the professional tutor or the head of department. All staff, both teaching and support, should be included in introductions and play an important role in welcoming new colleagues and making them feel at ease.

A sensible idea seen in the staffroom of a secondary school was a collection of head and shoulder photographs of all the staff and other colleagues who frequently visit the school. Names were printed under each photograph. New teachers and students often have difficulty putting a name to a face and this simple expedient would help to reduce anxiety. A set of Polaroid photographs would be cheap and easy to produce and to up-date whenever necessary.

Whole-school documentation to give to the newcomer

At the preliminary visit the new colleague or the trainee can be provided with a range of school documentation which can be perused at his or her leisure in order to be familiar with school organisation and processes. The quality of this documentation should be as high as possible and school managers should make sure that a thorough and detailed picture of all apects of school life can be easily referred to in school documentation as a crucial part of their staff development. When staff handbooks and notes for guidance are written they should be clearly laid out and appropriate for a 'mixed ability' audience who may or may not be familiar with the organisation of schools.

Documentation to give to newcomers would include: staff handbooks, survival guides for new staff, the school prospectus, whole-school policies, the calendar of meetings and events and a plan of the school. Health and safety information such as fire drill and first aid procedures should form part of written materials provided on induction.

The school induction programme

The professional tutor or INSET co-ordinator will most probably be responsible for the school programme and for ensuring that there are no overlaps and omissions between school, LEA and subject induction. In the case of the experienced teacher who joins the school at a middle management or senior level, the line manager should be responsible for induction and support. It is vital that whoever is organising an induction programme should be aware of the cycle of key events in the school such as report writing, parents' evenings and Records of Achievement so that newcomers are fully briefed well in advance of the event.

Newcomers will have different needs; the topic of needs assessment has already been introduced and will be expanded on below. It is important to remember when planning an induction programme that different categories of newcomer have different levels of knowledge and experience. For instance, a student on teaching practice comes with no previous teaching experience other than brief observation; a licensed or registered teacher who will be based in the school may be a completely 'blank slate' and induction has to start from scratch working with the other partners involved. Some trainers come from other sectors and some have already spent time as unqualified staff in schools and so have some idea of school organisation. A teacher trained overseas will arrive with a radically different set of preconceptions, skills and knowledge and a supply teacher will need very rapid induction to the actual mechanics of classroom and corridor life. A new head of year or department will be fully versed in the national educational framework but will need to know how to find his or her way around school and LEA procedures very quickly indeed.

Increasingly, resourced free time for induction purposes is becoming a luxury, especially as the probationary period is now abolished. This does not however reduce the actual need for induction and so, when inducting people who have a teaching timetable, schools will have to find time for presenting the modules listed in Figure 4.3 either in non-contact, INSET or directed time. Time is an issue not only for the person being inducted but also for the person/s delivering the induction, such as the mentor or the

Figure 4.3 *Modules for whole-school induction*

History of and background to the school	Decision-making structures
	Assessment and profiling
Discipline and support structures	Class management and control
Role of the tutor and year or house head	Meetings with peers
	Role of the head teacher
Role of the head of department or faculty	Whole-school policies
	Record keeping
Use of the library/resource area	Observation techniques
The list of effective teaching criteria	The role of the governing body
	Records of Achievement
How to evaluate your own progress and set targets	Rewards and sanctions
	SEN Code of Practice
Outside agencies, eg education social workers, police, educational psychologists	How children learn: language, marked aptitudes, race, gender
	Drug awareness
Child protection procedures	Community issues
LMS	Appraisal
Working with parents	Time management/directed time

Visits to other school, units and agencies.

Cross curricular themes: PSHE, information technology, citizenship, industrial and economic understanding, environmental awareness.

Industry links

Curriculum vitae and job applications

How the trainee will be assessed/appraised.

Future professional development.

(Modules to be selected according to the category of trainee).

professional tutor. In the best practice other post-holders in the school and the outside agencies working with the school are invited to give seminars or workshops to cover the relevant modules and a variety of styles should be used including lectures, workshops, action learning and seminars.

Departmental or subject-team induction

The mentor or supervisor will be responsible for induction at this level, in close co-operation with the professional tutor. In initial training the mentor will usually also work with partners from the LEA, HE and perhaps other schools.

Figure 4.4 shows the main elements of department or subject induction. They concentrate on subject-specific and classroom craft issues. Again, timing may be an important factor and categories of newcomer will not need exposure to all these modules.

Mentors and heads of department will greatly ease the induction of staff and students if they ensure that department handbooks and schemes of work are regularly up-dated giving a clear idea of coherence and progression. An A4 ring binder is the ideal format as it allows sections to be taken out and inserted whenever an up-date is needed. This can be done easily and quickly if the text is kept on a word processor file. There should be copies of handbooks and schemes of work readily available to all newcomers. Handbooks should contain job descriptions for the team, a list of resources and where they can be found, departmental policies with an obvious correlation to school policies, assessment and record-keeping procedures, useful addresses and telephone numbers for subject issues. Schemes of work should have detailed lesson or unit plans, incorporating homework and differentiated work.

The mentor should meet regularly with the newcomer (it helps if they have simultaneous non-contact time) and should make sure that s/he is assigned to a year or house group in order to acquire pastoral experience. Not only should the newcomer, where appropriate, be observed but s/he should be given the opportunity to observe the mentor and other experienced colleagues. Trainee teachers must be given the opportunity to visit and teach in other schools and it is certainly most beneficial for all newcomers to pay a visit to other schools in all phases and to different departments in the same school. The opportunity to shadow a pupil or a teacher is also invaluable. The mentor must ensure that the trainee is fully involved in the extra curricular life of the school by attendance at meetings and other functions.

If the newcomer is a student, the mentor will be responsible for setting up their timetable, by negotiation. In any case trainee teachers should have a gradual introduction to the teaching role, progressing from observation to team teaching and/or responsibility for a part of the lesson to a full load

Figure 4.4 *Elements of subject-team induction*

Departmental handbook	Seating plans for lessons
Access to resources and materials	Schemes of work
	National Curriculum
Differentiation	Lesson planning and preparation
Subject content	Subject teaching methods
Assessment and profiling	Discussion of college input
Actual observation	Debriefing and targets
Self-review and evaluation	Marking work
Visits outside the subject team	Discussion of assignments
Writing reports	Trainee's log or diary
Time for reflection	A special project, eg, preparation
Review of classes and pupils	of a unit of work
Mixed-ability teaching	Questioning techniques
Access to resources including I.T.	Making materials

of not more than 60 per cent of a normal timetable. Classes should cover a range of ages and abilities. Student teachers should be given some idea of their timetable when they make their preliminary visit to give them time to prepare. What the mentor should never do is use the trainee as another pair of hands, leaving him or her to sink or swim without preparation in the classroom and going off to work in an office or the staffroom. In the later stages of their training trainees will want to be autonomous and left in control of their classes but the mentor, mindful of the legal status of unqualified staff, should never be far away.

Mentor training: the core or generic processes

Subject- or phase-specific skills

This section deals with 'generic' mentoring processes, the core skills which all mentors in education need to develop. It must be emphasised that these 'generic' processes are not sufficient on their own to guarantee effective teacher training. Phase issues and subject-specific issues are perhaps even more important in the process of raising whole-school awareness about effective classroom delivery. The trainee primary school teacher needs to know a range of ways of managing the learning environment so that children work in groups and individually in an integrated way or in subject-specific areas. S/he will need to be familiar with the whole curriculum as well as all National Curriculum programmes of study and assessment techniques in Key Stages 1 and 2 as well as progression issues to Key Stage 3. The secondary school trainee will learn the classroom craft in an entirely subject-specific way and will need a detailed knowledge of the National Curriculum framework for that subject as well as having subject expertise at graduate or equivalent level. S/he will have to learn how to construct programmes of work in a spiral syllabus through Key Stages 3 and 4 for pupils of all abilities and must be thoroughly conversant with resources, methodology, assessment, progression issues, GCSE require-ment, A- and AS-level requirements as well as those of vocational courses such as GNVQ. All this will be in addition to whole-school issues, classroom management and organisation and pastoral matters.

Training in these core skills for school teachers is essential to the success of school-based teacher training and the development of the reflective practitioner. Furthermore, they are central to all management processes including the support and supervision of staff and pupils as well as appraisal. Schools which concentrate on them as a basis for their staff development programme will find a resulting improvement in teacher performance and pupil achievement. The processes are:

- assessing training needs;
- observation and assessment skills;
- giving and receiving positive and negative feedback;
- setting targets;
- counselling;
- negotiation and conflict solving.

Although these processes are dealt with separately the reader will see that they are inextricably interlinked. Training for one process will support all the others. The suggested approach relies upon the existence in the school of an agreed schedule of criteria of knowledge and skills for effective teaching as described above.

Assessing training needs

The content of the individual induction or training programme will depend on what the trainee already knows and what skills they already possess. The need for individually tailored induction programmes was emphasised in a DES letter to Chief Education Officers and other interested parties during the consultation relating to the schoolteacher probation issue (DES, 1991f). Special funding, said the letter, would be made available for such programmes. Readers will recall that assessing needs is the first step in the NCVQ Training and Development Lead Body framework for developing human potential. Too often our expectations and assumptions about what students and trainees already know or can do are too high. This has been confirmed by HMI in their surveys *The New Teacher in School* (DES, 1982; HMI, 1988) and also by teacher mentors in a variety of schemes.

There can be no assumption that teachers new to our schools all come with the same training needs. Although there is a core of knowledge and skills which applies to everyone there are differences of phase (nursery, primary, secondary, special, FE, etc.), status (standard scale, head of department or year, head teacher) and of previous educational background (trained in the UK, overseas) as well as of previous experience (abroad, not in the inner city, not recent, etc.). One of the entry criteria to the Newham primary licensed teacher scheme in 1990–1 has been 'All Licensed Teachers must be able to articulate the relationship of their previous learning to the primary curriculum'. Mentors on various schemes have highlighted the initial difficulties in their supervision due to their inability to grasp the different educational experience of their trainees and the ensuing mismatch of expectations. Needs analysis should therefore be an essential ingredient in all induction programmes and from the information gained a training and/or induction programme can be devised to suit the needs of each individual and to assist the mentor in their task. The resulting document/s can then form the beginning of a teaching profile or Record of Achievement if these are in use in a particular school. There are various ways of doing this and schools or team leaders will choose the means which best suit their organisation or their trainee/s.

Assignments or essays

Student teachers on conventional PGCE or BEd courses follow a structured course which allows time for assignments which can be informative for the school-based mentor when s/he has access to them. For instance the EP228 secondary initial teacher education course developed by the Open University which was used by some schemes for training licensed teachers set the following 1000-word assignment early in the course: 'Remembering your own education. What made your education a success?' Students were asked to refer to ethos, teachers' attitudes and relationships with pupils, behaviours and attitudes of adolescents, lesson content and methodology, home background, parental attitudes, social class, gender, ethnicity and other factors.

Journals

In addition, as part of the first unit in EP228 students were encouraged to '"look at yourself, your past and what assumptions you make when you begin to teach" which you can continue to use not just throughout this course, or your initial training course as a whole, but into the early years of your career'. The main vehicle for this was the journal which they were asked to keep. The emphasis on both past and current experiences was intended to stimulate reflection. In the Thames Polytechnic/Tower Hamlets Articled teacher scheme (Thames Polytechnic, 1990b) this journal was called the 'Professional Development Log' and forms part of the students' portfolio which also contains records of observations and enquiries, details of planning and resourcing, pupil case study, etc.

The use of observation and discussion

In the observation phase of the Newham primary licensed teachers' scheme, trainees were given a day in Newham schools simply to observe. The aim of the exercise was to give a quick impression of what British inner city primary schools are like. The licensed teachers then discussed what they saw and how it differed from their own expectations with college tutors at a seminar. College staff felt that having the school mentors present at the same time would give them a very helpful insight into the assumptions, expectations and needs of their students. This system could easily be replicated for students in other induction schemes. Time factors for most new colleagues who have to teach full timetables will render this unrealistic unless INSET time is set aside. There are other methods which can be quickly achieved.

The application form

Candidates for posts could be asked to describe their previous experience as part of their application. It would be necessary to stipulate on the form that this information would be used to identify training needs so that candidates understand that this particular information would not be treated confidentially.

Interviews or line management meetings

Time could be set aside by the mentor or supervisor to discuss previous experience of and assumptions about education with the trainee in the first formal meeting. It would be helpful if this could follow a day of observing the school, perhaps by shadowing a pupil or a teacher.

Questionnaires or check-lists used diagnostically

This is obviously the most depersonalised method and can either be used as the only system of needs analysis, or more usefully with any of the methods described above. The mentor, comparing the information gained against a check-list, can then devise a composite picture of the development needs of the trainee from which an individual training programme can be drawn up using aspects of LEA and school induction and also supervision and practical work in the school. If the part of the check-list which relates to teaching skills is also being used for observation and assessment (see section below) then the new colleague and the mentor are working to a consistent and coherent set of standards which enables targets to be set at every stage and reflection on progress to be made by both the mentor and the trainee. Alternatively, the check-list sent to new colleagues with induction documentation could be amended. Self-assessment is an important ingredient in the development of any professional skills. The Oxfordshire Internship scheme used its list of important abilities for this purpose and the Hertfordshire Licensed Teacher scheme which grew out of the HATS scheme developed a set of criteria to be used formatively in this way.

Whatever the nature of the instrument or list of criteria used, lesson observation is an intrinsic part of any needs assessment, self-assessment, training or appraisal programme; successful observation techniques are enlarged upon in the next section.

Observation and assessment skills

Reflection on teaching skills through observation

Lesson observation is such a vital part of the development and assessment of teaching skills that both trainee and mentor need to receive careful training and preparation early in the school-based period in order to ensure that observation is truly developmental. As one author puts it: 'Without training many observers look but do not see' (Montgomery, 1984, p 14). Schools in partnership with HE institutions who perhaps have agreed arrangements whereby lecturers do their 'recent and relevant' teaching practice in the school would benefit greatly from their expertise in lesson observation should consultancy or training be offered by these colleagues.

Not only will the mentor be observing the trainee and through the feedback given allowing him or her to test developing ideas, but more importantly the trainee will spend a great deal of time observing the mentor and others. The first stages of initial school-based and school-centred teacher training will be spent almost entirely observing. For many this will be their first contact with the classroom since their school days and it represents a transitional period the importance of which cannot be over-estimated. It is where the teaching and relationship patterns for an entire career will begin to be formulated. It is up to the mentor to ensure that observation by the trainee is not simply a boring and endless series of lessons to be sat in and that it is used as a constructive, coherent and focused element in the training programme.

Lesson observation is also used for and by qualified teachers, for instance in the support and assessment of newly qualified teachers. This continues to happen even though statutory probationary period has disappeared, as schools want to ensure that pupils are receiving the best possible teaching from young recruits to the profession and to help new teachers do their job without constraints. Many school managers also find it useful to negotiate a programme of observation of colleagues who are not newly qualified. When this is done in a careful and supportive way as described below, teachers find it stimulating and useful. For senior managers it provides a structured way to be out and about in the classroom and to write positive comments on references and testimonials. It is also an essential part of school teacher appraisal.

Working in partnership

'Moving schools' are those where an ethos of collaboration prevails. (Rosenholz, 1989) All observation involves a contract between the observer and the observed and so is a good way of developing team-work skills. Many schools use peer observation by experienced teachers as a cost-effective and practical form of staff development where paired volunteers observe each other teach and discuss the results of the observation in order to enhance good teaching practice in both parties. Where licensed teachers or students are paired in schools, peer group observation is also a sensible form of development and collaboration. Shadowing experienced teachers or pupils for a day is also a useful form of observation which, like all forms, needs careful preparation.

It is not good practice to throw students 'in at the deep end' and part of the transition from observation to teaching full classes can be team teaching: taking a part of the lesson or a specific group of pupils. This involves observation by both the mentor and the trainee and so the comments on planning lesson observation apply equally to team teaching. As the trainee becomes more autonomous the balance in the partnership shifts.

Some teachers do not like being observed. They feel threatened by having an 'outsider' in the room. Training in observation skills and thorough planning should minimise the opposition encountered in a minority of cases and help everyone to be comfortable in the role of observer and observed.

Styles of lesson observation

There are two main kinds of lesson observation. The first is the 'clinical' supervision style which has been traditionally used by teacher trainers or those assessing teaching performance in schools: senior managers and inspectors. In the clinical observation all the power lies with the observer or supervisor. It is didactic in that the person being observed has no say in what the focus of the observation should be. The observer adopts the 'fly on the wall' position, usually at the back of the room, and does not intervene in the lesson. This form of supervision can be used very sympathetically but it does not involve the person being observed in reflective action until the very end of the process, after feedback has been given. It is suitable for formal assessment of teaching skill.

The other style of lesson observation is 'partnership' or 'democratic' supervision in which the observer adopts a counselling style. The student or teacher is able to explore and articulate issues of concern by negotiating the focus of the observation in advance of the lesson and being able to reflect on the agreed issues with the help of the mentor. Evidently students in the early stages of their training require a great deal more assistance with the selection of content and focus for observations than do experienced teachers and it is the mentor's role to guide and advise them. This style is co-operative and developmental and is particularly suited to peer group observation and to observation of trainees when no formal assessment is being made but as part of the coaching process carried out by the mentor. Partnership supervision can still involve a formal contract between the observer and the observed.

Supervisors will find themselves using a combination of these two styles at different stages in the training programme.

Planning the observation

This section concentrates on democratic supervision but many of the points made are apposite for clinical supervision, as will be obvious. The stages for planning an observation are:

- the student identifies an aspect of teaching skill for the focus
- s/he discusses the focus with the mentor at a planning meeting
- ways of obtaining feedback on the focus are agreed
- teaching/observing/note taking takes place
- evidence is discussed in a post-lesson conference
- a new focus is identified and the cycle begins again (Mercer and Abbott, 1989).

The essential ingredients of this process are:

- time and a quiet setting for a planning meeting
- a set of clearly defined criteria for effective teaching, possibly adapted as an observation evaluation form
- the focus of the observation
- the style of the observation
- the form of the written record taken during the observation
- feedback given as soon as possible
- time and a quiet setting for feedback
- setting targets for positive action in the next stage.

Choosing a focus

Appendix 12 gives a model format for evaluating teaching performance which, if the guidelines in this book are used, would follow naturally from the school's set of criteria. The outcomes described in the pro forma are divided into broad domains, and students or teachers could choose any one of these as a focus for the observation. Students are usually overwhelmingly concerned with questions of discipline and control. Alternatively, the trainee may need advice on a particular class that is proving difficult or may want the mentor to see a lesson with a group which is progressing well.

Different criteria apply if the observation is for learning (the student observes) or developing (the mentor observes.) Both parties also need to discuss environmental and social factors affecting the lesson such as room constraints, issues in the local area, the pupil 'profile' including age, ability and specific individuals where necessary.

Other possible foci are:

- questioning and answering techniques
- race and gender issues
- the nature of pupil talk
- ways of bringing and keeping pupils on task
- use of resources
- time pupils spend 'on task'
- non-verbal communication

Observing the lesson

Armed with the results of the pre-planning and carrying his or her evaluation sheet, the observer arrives at the lesson. S/he will have agreed in advance with the person being observed whether to sit unobtrusively at the back, or in a suitable position which will not distract pupils' attention or whether to participate in the lesson. Another decision to be made is how the observer is going to be introduced to pupils, if at all. If the observer is not going to participate in the lesson then s/he must not intervene at all costs, except in situations where safety is at risk. Another quandary felt by observers, especially if they are inexperienced, is whether to avoid eye contact with pupils and teacher. It is of course perfectly all right to give a friendly smile – this sets everyone at ease.

The 'halo' effect occurs during lesson observation when pupil behaviour is better than normal due to the presence and/or status of the observer. When this happens a false impression of the trainee's relationships and class control can sometimes be gained. As a head teacher the writer is only too aware of the 'halo' effect but less experienced observers should take it into account.

Recording the observation

Video is used extensively in student and mentor or supervisor training to record lessons and the subsequent debriefing. Where both parties are willing this can be a valuable exercise in schools especially in peer observation. Tape recordings can be used equally well to enable the teacher or student to reflect on use of language, voice projection, questioning techniques, interruptions and a range of other factors.

In the majority of cases the report will be written, although trainee and mentor may agree on occasion to give a verbal report. Be that as it may, students do value having a written report of an observation which helps enormously in the process of reflective action.

Appendix 12 provides a model observation evaluation sheet, which is extremely detailed and covers all aspects of classroom behaviour. Observers may choose to use that format to write a lesson profile based on the agreed focus (see above).

In addition, a script or blow-by-blow account of the lesson which the observer scribbles furiously during the observation is enormously helpful for use during the debriefing and to give the teacher or student an objective view of everything that happened, including things that s/he may not have noticed at the time. In a script of this kind it is very important to distinguish between real fact (which is preferable), inference and personal comment. The debriefing and feedback must be based on observable fact. A typical script would begin like this:

Thursday October 31, period 3: Ms X and 9M English.

10:05   You are waiting for the class as I arrive. The room is tidy and the date and title are written on the board. Pupil folders are out on the desks.

10:06   The class begins to arrive and you show them in. They take their seats with a little chat. Deidre asks you about homework and while you are answering Garry and Abdul arrive. You do not ask them why they are late. There are 25 pupils present. All the boys are sitting together.

10:09   Register. (Samantha still has her coat on.) 'Right, today we're going to finish our projects on "Flat Stanley". Who can remember what we did in the last lesson?'

And so on.

Giving and receiving positive and negative feedback

This is a very important management process and training for it will not only assist mentors in their role but will make management more effective.

A discussion after any observation is vital and where the trainee has taken the lesson it enables both trainee and mentor to reflect and evaluate, to see how previously agreed targets have been met and to set new ones. This cannot be stressed strongly enough. *The quality of the feedback is the single most important factor in improving performance.* The type or number of the criteria for assessment, the nature of the written record, the style of the observation and the agreed focus are all rendered meaningless if the mentor does not give constructive and developmental feedback.

The setting for the feedback and its timing are important. Immediately after the lesson it is good practice to thank the person observed and give a few words of praise and encouragement. Set a time for a formal feedback if this has not already been done. Ideally it should take place no longer than two days later. A quiet and relaxing room should be used where there will be no interruptions. The general principle is that giving negative feedback in public settings like the staffroom is always inappropriate.

Everyone should find it easy to give positive feedback or praise (although our colleagues or our pupils may not feel that we do so with sufficient regularity). We find it less easy, and even distasteful, to give criticism or negative feedback in a misguided attempt not to demotivate the other party or to hurt their feelings.

There are ways to make it easier and less threatening. Use positive and warm verbal and non-verbal communication. Make eye contact and smile. Avoid raised voices and pointing fingers, or hands on hips, which are classic examples of confrontational body language. Listen sympathetically and genuinely to the trainee and try not to interrupt.

It helps when negative feedback is tempered with some praise. Except in the most extreme cases this is easy. Discuss all the things which went well however obvious they may seem. This enables the person receiving the feedback to feel that a balanced view is being given and that their performance has been valued.

Next, stick to fact rather than opinion. The value of the written script and pro forma becomes apparent in this context. The school's list of criteria for effective teaching can also be used in this way, with both parties running through each relevant item.

The use of open-ended questions which elicit a frank response from the trainee is much better than proferring bald statements. 'How do you feel it went?' usually receives an honest and thoughtful answer and may mean that you do not have to raise painful issues yourself.

Possibly the mentor is the recipient of negative feedback and there are techniques for dealing with it which can serve to defuse conflict. The points given above about use of verbal and body language apply here also. Accept the feedback at face value and if possible welcome it by saying something like, 'Thank you for those comments, I shall certainly bear them in mind'. Make sure this is genuinely meant. It does not help to counter-attack with statements like, 'You've got a nerve to say that considering you've only been here for five minutes' or calling the other person's competence into question (even if justified). Nor should you justify your position with comments such as, 'Well, I had to intervene in your lesson because Gary was running rings round you'.

What you can do is clarify and explore: 'Let me clarify why I took over at that point . . .', then illustrate your position by referring to facts. Alternatively you can suggest, 'Let's explore together my reasons for stepping in at that point'. This approach is suggesting to the other party that you had objective, justifiable and neutral reasons for your action.

Setting targets

This is the final stage in the observation cycle and also is a process in its own right which should inform all stages of training and supervision. It is as essential to the process of enabling 'reflection in action' as is the skill of giving feedback. Both the mentor and the trainee should be able to identify strengths and weaknesses in teaching skills, although as already stated, students need more help with this at the start of their training. Mentors comment on how the process of helping trainees to set targets has had a beneficial effect on their professional development, as they have been obliged to examine their own practice.

The check-list or list of criteria adopted by the school can be a sharp focus for joint identification of strengths and weaknesses in the debriefing session. Similarly, if a different focus has been agreed in advance the student will have a clear idea of whether the target has been met. If this is not the case the mentor, using the recorded data in the observation record, can raise the issue. Setting targets for improvement will then follow naturally. At the next formal meeting the trainee and the mentor can discuss to what extent targets have been met.

Setting one's own targets as part of the learning and training programme outside the process of lesson observation is also necessary for the trainee. The line management agenda given in Appendix 8 shows how target setting is a natural element in support and supervision of staff as well as in appraisal. It also features as an element in school review, drawing up development plans and the management of change. Most often, where there is a regular agenda for discussion rather than an unstructured informal chat the teacher or student comes to the meeting prepared in advance with targets to be achieved.

In the Light of Torches, the guidelines for the pilot appraisal scheme in Suffolk, gives a clear definition for setting targets which can be adapted to any situation:

> Targets to improve teaching effectiveness should be specific, realistic, challenging, achievable and commensurate with the resources available. They should be limited in number (3–5), clear on both the teacher's plans for achievement and the intended result (Suffolk Education Department, 1987, p 22).

It has already been indicated that the 'generic' mentoring skills are all inter-related. Target or goal setting is one of the three stages in the counselling method called 'effective helping'. We now move on to consider counselling as a mentoring process.

Counselling

The skills associated with counselling are imperative to successful mentoring. There are various models, one of the most common being the Egan approach to effective helping which is extensively documented in books by the originator, Gerard Egan (1982, 1986). His model describes the three stages of counselling as:

- Identifying and clarifying problem situations and unused opportunities.
- Goal setting – developing a more desirable scenario.
- Action – moving toward the preferred scenario.

Integral to the process is the concept of 'client self-responsibility' which is strengthened by success, modelling, encouragement and reducing fear or anxiety. There are obvious links between the concept of 'self-responsibility' and that of the 'reflective practitioner' and the relationship between these skills and the need for the mentor to enable the trainee teacher to reflect on his/her own practice and thus progress in a developmental fashion is self-evident. Mentors trained in counselling techniques are enthusiastic about the improvement in their management skills and relationships with other colleagues, with pupils and with parents.

Egan (1982, p 35ff.) lists the skills that helpers need for each stage as follows:

Stage 1: Empathy indicated through good posture and eye contact and avoiding negative or distracting behaviour.

Active listening: listening to both the verbal and non-verbal messages of the speaker however confused.

Responding by showing you have listened carefully and have understood.

Probing in order to help the client be more specific about what is bothering him or her. 'I'm not sure just what is the problem here' is an example of an open ended question that you can use.

Foundational qualities are not exactly skills but are qualities which form the basis of helping. They are: responsiveness, being openly supportive, maintaining confidentiality, refraining from manipulation, respecting the client's values even when they differ from your own and showing respect.

Stage 2: The ability to analyse the data the client presents.

Being able to challenge: helping the client develop new and more useful perpsectives by sharing information, confrontation leading to self understanding, sharing your own experiences with the client and immediacy (exploring the here and now of the client helper relationship).

Goal setting skills: helping the client to set achievable goals based on the exploration of the problem and then helping them to move from declarations of intent to action.

Stage 3: Programme development skills: the means chosen to translate targets into action. The mentor will help the client identify and choose a course of action.

Helping the client prepare themselves for the course of action by anticipating problems and providing challenge and support.

Helping clients to ask themselves three evaluative questions:
Is the client participating fully?
Is the goal being achieved?
Are the goals appropriate to the situation?

Negotiation and conflict solving

These skills are closely related to counselling although there are some differences in emphasis.

The mentor needs to negotiate constantly with the trainee and with other partners in the training process. These can include college staff, senior management, teachers in other schools and other departments or even the trainee him or herself. Some of the issues for negotiation can be delicate and the opportunities for conflict are legion. For instance, one of the major difficulties in the application of school-based teacher training is in the tension which can arise between the mentor's role as 'critical friend' and supporter and that of assessor and examiner. Although this can be minimised when responsibilities between the mentor and other partners are clearly defined, it is not unknown for personality clashes or conflicts between mentor and trainee to occur. Finely tuned negotiation skills are therefore necessary and training is essential. It is also useful to bear in mind that teachers often meet conflict in their daily work. Skills for solving conflict are also a very important attribute for the successful manager either at head teacher or classroom teacher level and as with counselling skills can dramatically improve relationships with pupils, parents and staff.

The basic skills of good negotiation are very similar to those needed for counselling: anticipating and avoiding possible conflict, non-confrontational verbal or body language, good verbal and non-verbal communication, choosing appropriate settings for the negotiation to take place, clearly identifying and separating issues, the ability to review and summarise the other person's points, acknowledging the value of the other person's point of view and identifying issues of agreement.

The negotiator must also remember some key principles which can also be applied to counselling and giving feedback. Everyone must be equally involved in solving the problem. Mentors need to be trained to take the following formal steps involved in solving a conflict, should it arise, in a positive way which is seen to be fair:

• Describe the situation and review previous discussions.
• Ask for reasons for the situation in order to clarify.
• Listen and respond with empathy.
• Indicate unambiguously what action you must take and why.
• Agree on specific action and follow up date.
• Indicate your confidence in the parties involved.
  (Development Dimension, 1984).

Conclusion

The aim of this book has been to provide a rationale for raising teacher performance both in the practice of classroom craft and in management skills by using the training of teachers as a framework for school-based staff development. Teacher training should be seen as a continuous process which begins with the teacher's own education, carries on through initial training and is continued throughout a teacher's professional life.

The new routes into teaching which have arisen from the shortage of teachers and the high staff turnover in some areas as well as the shift in emphasis on both sides of the political spectrum toward school-based teacher training, make it imperative for schools to look closely at the quality and consistency of the training they provide. Most secondary schools are now involved in either school-based or school-centred initial teacher training.

Therefore the practical aspects of training are acquiring an apparently greater significance than the theoretical basis, whether because of a developing interest in 'apprenticeship' models of training or because of an increasing assumption that the trainers should be themselves active practitioners. The role of the school-based mentor as the trainer is gaining in importance due to this assumption. The theoretical side of teacher training cannot be eliminated if training is to encourage reflective practice in both mentor and trainee. This is being demonstrated in new and radical partnerships which are springing up between schools and their colleagues in HE to deliver PGCE and licensed teacher training in a way which reflects a more equal balance between schools and HE institutions and in the school-centred schemes. The greater autonomy for schools provided through LMS and Grant Maintained status also lays emphasis on the need for schools to take the lead in devising their own training programmes either on their own or with partners in the training process.

In such schools the whole-school ethos must be geared towards effective teaching performance and the training necessary to give every teacher at whichever stage in their career the opportunity to reflect upon and improve their own practice. The concept of the 'reflective' practitioner is very familiar to teacher trainers but less explicitly contained in school development processes. Schools which concentrate on developing 'reflection in action' through the core mentoring processes will enable their staff to be more effective in a range of other school management processes as well as being better teachers. In addition to the core skills needed for teacher training, schools can focus on how to transmit to students and new teachers subject-specific content and methods in a coherent framework which should improve the classroom experience for pupils. Such a focus also greatly increases mentor awareness of subject pedagogy.

Schools which use teacher training as the basis for staff development must ensure that the whole school is involved in the development of policy and process. Without across-the-board participation, consistency of performance, training and expectation cannot be guaranteed. The first stage is to carry out an audit of training expertise in the school by surveying middle managers and new or trainee teachers. Their views and opinions expressed in the results of the structured questionnaires will be very informative. The questionnaire also helps to set out clear expectations to all middle managers about induction and training.

Communication systems need to be in place which will ensure that information about training is carried to all who need to know it, from senior management to standard scale teachers. This means that if teacher training is a priority it will feature as such in the school development plan and there will be clear policies in school documentation about teacher training for the different categories of students and trainees. Job descriptions will be needed for those who are responsible for training: from the professional tutor to the subject mentor. Monitoring and evaluation procedures must be in place to make sure that accountability to student and pupil is taken seriously. Awareness will also be raised by whole-school debate about the criteria needed for effective teaching. Despite the fact that there is a core of criteria which are needed for all good teaching, whatever the phase or subject, the final list will differ from school to school.

Schools now hold the 'balance of power' in making choices about how they use resources and which partners they will work with. Single schools or clusters will be able to choose between LEAs, HE institutions and independent consultants and trainers. Apart from the statutory duties retained by LEAs, should they survive, all these partners will be competing to sell the same kind of training packages to schools. These packages could cover induction for new teachers, mentor training, peer group workshops for mentors and trainees and supervision for mentors. In addition there is a real future for schools as 'training schools', either in collaboration with HE or not, and there are mutual benefits for all partners to do with accreditation, resourcing and the sharing of expertise.

The key role in school-based and school-centred teacher training is taken by the mentor. A variety of definitions of this function have been given and it has been argued that mentoring skills are useful to all managers and trainers. The benefits of mentoring for schools and individual teachers have been highlighted as well as some of the problems, which can be avoided through careful planning and training. Some pointers for the selection of mentors have been provided and the question of mentor training has been examined. Mentor training is increasingly being 'sold' by teacher trainers from HE, but LEA personnel could offer the same service. The training should consist of the opportunity to develop the ability to articulate subject-specific theory, content and methodology as well as certain generic skills.

It is important for middle managers to be aware of these issues as training is an important part of the support and supervision of their teams. Schools may be interested in investigating standards provided by National Vocational Qualifications in training and development to use as the rationale for the training function of middle managers. In sectors other than school teaching these standards are leading to qualifications and there is room for the development of qualifications in mentoring.

Middle managers will also be directly involved in the whole-school debate about means of defining and assessing effective teaching. Should broad areas be used or detailed check-lists of measurable criteria? Both have a variety of uses. It is up to the school to decide and by doing so set expectations.

The induction of trainees is a vital part of the training of student and experienced teachers and there needs to be coherence between the induction offered by the LEA, the school and the department. Clearly defined responsibilities within partnerships will help avoid overlap or omissions.

Middle managers will also receive or deliver mentor training in schools. This will consist of:

- subject-specific skills;
- the assessment of needs;
- observation skills;
- giving and receiving feedback;
- target setting;
- counselling;
- negotiation and conflict solving.

The development of such skills should be part of the training of all middle managers and appraisers. Training schools should then raise achievement across the board because of the interdependence of mentoring and the management and support of staff and pupils.

The final part of this book provides practical assistance to all those interested in training others or themselves to work in schools. The appendices contain model policies and documents which schools can copy or modify and the bibliography gives a list of texts for those who wish to pursue the topic further, either fleetingly or in depth.

Appendices

Introduction

The obvious purpose of Appendices 1 and 2 is to enable school managers to locate where the teacher training expertise is in the school by asking certain questions of middle managers (trainers and potential trainers) as well as those colleagues who are receiving or have recently received induction or training. A secondary result of the questionnaires is the improved consistency of good practice by the mere exercise of filling in the forms. Trainees gain a better idea of what to expect and ask for and middle managers are given a clear indication of what is expected of them. Finally, the new ideas expressed by those filling in the forms can provide useful additions to training programmes in the school.

A whole-school policy on teaching practice in initial teacher training given in Appendix 3 is an example which can be modified to cover other forms of training such as induction, licensed teacher training etc. As with Appendices 1 and 2, it serves both to inform and to set out what would be expected of colleagues at different levels of seniority who collaborate in training. It should be published in the school handbook and regularly monitored in review, line management and appraisal meetings.

Appendix 4 is a check-list which is particularly helpful to team leaders (especially those who are relatively new to the role) responsible for students on teaching practice. It can also provide guidance for the student, giving some idea of what the training programme should consist of. Appendix 5 illustrates additional items which can be added to the check-list for other categories of trainee.

Appendices 6 and 7 provide model job descriptions, the former for the professional tutor (in some schools called teacher tutor or INSET co-ordinator) and the latter for the subject mentor. It is important for responsibilities to be clearly defined to everyone in the school and for the benefit of partners from outside. Job descriptions are essential in this respect for setting out expectations, providing objective criteria for selection and also for monitoring and appraisal. Not included here but complementary to these two examples would be paragraphs in the job descriptions of team leaders setting out their training responsibilities.

Appendix 8 is a fairly standard line management agenda which facilitates two-way communication, regular feedback and monitoring. The questions given here are also central to the agenda of most school teacher appraisal interviews. They cover all aspects of the middle and senior managers' role, which of course includes all phases of teacher training.

The List of Important Abilities from the Oxfordshire Internship scheme given in Appendix 9 is just one of many possible examples of lists of broad competences which attempt to define effective teaching for the purpose of training, information and assessment. This particular list is in contrast to the narrowly mechanistic check-lists used in some schemes in the USA and elsewhere. Section 2 is particularly interesting in that it defines effectiveness in terms of pupil outcome.

Following on from this, Appendix 10 is a summary of all the broad categories or domains listed in a wide variety of assessment schemes attempting to define criteria for good teaching. It is a useful starting point for schools seeking to construct their own list or pro forma (such as the observation sheet given in Appendix 12). It does not claim to be exhaustive.

Appendix 11 is a document from the history section of the Oxfordshire Internship scheme which shows how a broad domain can be broken down into measurable criteria, in this case section 2 of the list of important abilities.

Appendix 12 shows how individual criteria developed from broad domains (given in the section headings) can be used to assess performance and to provide a focus for lesson observation, planning, discussion and feedback as well as setting targets for future development. The pro forma can be used as a training instrument as well as part of the appraisal cycle.

APPENDIX 1: TRAINING AUDIT QUESTIONNAIRE FOR TRAINEES AND NEW STAFF

THE SCHOOL AS A TRAINING ESTABLISHMENT: AUDIT OF _____ SCHOOL

NAME (optional) _____

Please return to _____ by _____

Thank you very much for your time.

1. Are you a student?   YES/NO
   an NQT this year?   YES/NO
   recently qualified?   YES/NO
   a new teacher from 'out-county'?   YES/NO
   an overseas-trained teacher?   YES/NO
   any other category? (please specify) _____

2. Do you know who is your 'mentor' or supervisor in your department?   YES/NO
   2.1 Is it the head of department?   YES/NO
   2.2 Someone else?   YES/NO

3. Do you know who is in charge of training in the school?   YES/NO

4. Will these persons be assessing your performance as well as giving guidance?
   Department mentor   YES/NO
   School mentor   YES/NO

5. Were you given access to the following:
   5.1 School induction   YES/NO
   5.2 Department induction   YES/NO
   5.3 School documentation   YES/NO
   5.4 Department documentation   YES/NO
   5.5 Pastoral training   YES/NO
   5.6 Extra-curricular activities   YES/NO
   5.7 Time for induction   YES/NO
   5.8 Opportunity for discussion (please specify)   YES/NO
   5.9 Support and guidance (please specify)   YES/NO
   5.10 Whole-school policies   YES/NO
   5.11 Opportunities to observe others   YES/NO
   5.12 Opportunities to be observed   YES/NO

5.13 Opportunities for team teaching   YES/NO
5.14 Regular guidance/feedback   YES/NO
5.15 Opportunities to set targets   YES/NO
5.16 Help with lesson planning   YES/NO

6. What in your opinion were the strengths of departmental induction? _____

_____

7. What in your opinion were its weaknesses? _____

8. What in your opinion were the strengths of school induction? _____

9. What in your opinion were its weaknesses? _____

10. What elements could usefully be added to department induction? _____

11. What could usefully be added to school induction? _____

Appendix 2: Training Audit Questionnaire for Middle Managers

THE SCHOOL AS A TRAINING ESTABLISHMENT: AUDIT OF SCHOOL

Questionnaire for senior and middle managers.

	This year	Previous years
1. Do you have experience of supervising trainees:		
1.1 Student teachers	Yes/No	Yes/No
1.2 NQTs	Yes/No	Yes/No
1.3 Overseas teachers	Yes/No	Yes/No
1.4 Out-county teachers	Yes/No	Yes/No
1.5 Other trainees (Please specify)	Yes/No	Yes/No

2. Please give some idea of numbers supervised:

	This year	Previous years
1.1		
1.2		
1.3		
1.4		
1.5		

3. What training have you received for this task either in school or elsewhere?

4. Do you feel confident about assuming responsibility for trainees?   Yes/No.
   4.1 Can you say why?

5. What do you regard as your own strengths as a mentor/supervisor?

6. What do you regard as your own weaknesses as a mentor/supervisor?

7. What do you regard as strengths in the school's system in this respect?

8. What do you regard as weaknesses in the school's system in this respect?

9. Do you delegate the role of mentor/supervisor to anyone else in your team?   YES/NO

10. If the answer to question 9 was 'yes' what training and support do you give the mentor/supervisor?

11. Is your training role specified clearly in your job description or that of anyone on your team?

12. Does your cluster, department or year have a specific induction programme for trainees or new teachers?

YES/NO

   (If 'yes', please append details).

13. What documentation does your cluster, department or year give to trainees and new teachers? (Please append details)

14. How much time do you or others on your team spend on training and supervising trainees and new teachers?
   - 14.1 Induction prior to arrival _____
   - 14.2 Induction on arrival _____
   - 14.3 Discussion of school policies _____
   - 14.4 Discussion of classroom management _____
   - 14.5 Discussion of lesson preparation _____
   - 14.6 Team teaching _____
   - 14.7 Mutual observation _____
   - 14.8 Evaluation of performance _____
   - 14.9 Target setting _____
   - 14.10 Other activities _____

15. How much encouragement do you give to trainees to participate in extra-curricular activities?

Name (optional) _____

Please return to _____

by _____

APPENDIX 3: MODEL OF WHOLE-SCHOOL POLICY ON SCHOOL-BASED INITIAL TEACHER TRAINING

This policy can easily be adapted to suit the needs of other categories of trainee and would operate in conjunction with partnership agreement jointly signed by head/ governors and HE institution.

1. *Placement of student teachers in departments*
This is the joint responsibility of the school and the teacher training institution according to the partnership agreement. Criteria for successful placement would be:

   1.1 Effective liaison between all partners.
   1.2 Appropriate funding arrangements.
   1.3 A suitably staffed subject department – with an ethos conducive to successful training.
   1.4 Suitably qualified subject mentor/s.
   1.5 A whole-school approach to training.
   1.6 The placement in the school of agreed numbers of student teachers in the said subject specialising in pairs or groups.

2. *Responsibilities in school*
The school must ensure that these are clearly defined and known to everyone.

   2.1 *Head/Governors*
   Annual review and signing of the partnership. Monitoring income and expenditure. Development planning in consultation with whole school.

   2.2 *Professional tutor/INSET coordinator*
   Implementation of school policy. Liaison with training partners. Coordination of placements. Dissemination of information and effective communication, bearing in mind the needs of all parties. Coordination of practical training for mentors and students on local, national and general issues. Coordination of training budgets including liaison with school timetabler on mentor release.

   2.3 *Heads of department or faculty*
   Day-to-day support and supervision of students on TP – although this responsibility may be delegated to mentors. Participation in final assessment of the student in consultation with the mentor and the HE staff. Resolving difficulties between mentors and students.

   2.4 *The mentor*
   Day-to-day professional support of the student. Translation of theoretical studies into practice in liaison with the validating institution. Giving advice and guidance on professional and classroom issues. Providing information on the practical aspects of subject content, teaching

methods, training issues and school procedures. Assessing the student's needs and devising a training programme in consultation with him/her to include observation, visits, meetings, teaching and time for reflection. Removing any constraints which may hinder the student's progress. With the validating institution and the HOD, formal assessment of the student. In order to perform these duties, the mentor needs free time with the student, to be paid for from partnership funding, of a minimum of one lesson per week.

3. *School induction*

School personnel need to be aware that this may be the student's first contact with a school since their own schooldays.

3.1 The student should visit the school before the teaching practice on at least one occasion and for a minimum period of one day.

3.2 S/he should be given all relevant school and department documentation (see Appendix 4).

3.3 S/he should be given a tour of the school and of the department and be introduced to key staff.

3.4 The timetable, any special project and a calendar for the school practice should be discussed to allow for preparation by mentor and student. This will include all school and university days, key dates, divisions of responsibility between school and HE staff, deadlines for written work and projects.

3.5 The early programme of observation should be organised during the pre-visit and the rationale behind lesson observation clearly explained and discussed. This should include observing lessons by other teachers in other departments or in other schools and following pupils or teachers for a day.

3.6 The student's application forms containing personal and educational details should be received by the mentor prior to the first visit to allow training needs to be identified. (*Note:* The establishment of mental and physical fitness to teach by candidates for the teaching profession and the search of police records are the responsibility of the validating body: the university or college in school-based, and the school in school-centred initial training.

3.7 The mentor should make school and department expectations clear to facilitate the student's induction into the professional role.

3.8 Introductions should be made to other students and NQTs based in the school.

4. *Timetable*

4.1 This should allow time to complete any college projects and to reflect on the school experience. A gradual build-up to approximately 60 per cent of a full teaching load should be the norm.

4.2 Students should have contact with a wide range of ages and abilities in their teaching practice.

4.3 The school experience for a student should begin with observation and progress to team teaching with the class teacher and/ or responsibility for a part of the lesson, moving gradually to taking full responsibility.

4.4 A trainee should have timetabled free time with his/her mentor.

5. *Assessment*

5.1 Responsibility for the assessment of the student's teaching practice should be clearly established.

5.2 Criteria should be agreed in advance between all partners including the student.

5.3 Where doubt exists about any aspect of the student's performance, this should be discussed between all partners at regular intervals in order to agree supportive action or otherwise.

5.4 Regular observation of teaching and an interim report will help alert all parties to any difficulties.

5.5 All observation and reports should be negotiated and discussed with the student in advance. It is helpful if the student or mentor suggests a focus for the observation.

5.6 There should be a written record of all observations.

5.7 Feedback based on factual data gathered during the observation should be given very briefly at the end of the lesson and in greater detail, in a private setting, within 24 hours to enable the opportunity for self-evaluation and the setting of targets.

6. *Support and supervision during the school practice*

6.1 The mentor/supervisor/class teacher must transfer responsibility for the class gradually and should be available at all times. This is essential during practical activities with pupils which involve health and safety risks.

6.2 Teaching timetables should provide a balance of age and ability.

6.3 In addition to informal day-to-day contacts, regular meetings with the student should be timetabled to discuss lesson preparation, any problems which may arise, focused observation and linking practice with college input.

6.4 The mentor should have formal weekly meetings with the student in addition to informal day-to-day contact. Topics for discussion at early meetings will include: needs assessment, relating college work to school practice, organisation of the student's time, discussion of written and practical assignments, general feedback.

6.5 Mentors should be allowed time to meet as a group and with the professional tutor.

7. *The wider professional role*

Students should be involved in the wider role of the teacher:

- contractual obligations
- attendance and punctuality
- preparation for further professional development/advancement
- attachment to a pastoral group
- attendance at department, year, staff and parents' meetings
- involvement in social and extracurricular events
- school policies and documentation
- INSET days
- outside agencies
- preparation of a unit of work or special project to be used in the department and to be negotiated at the pre-visit.

APPENDIX 4: EXAMPLE OF A CHECK-LIST TO BE USED BY SCHOOLS TO FACILITATE THE INDUCTION AND SUPERVISION OF STUDENT TEACHERS

This checklist is based on one produced by The Village College, Comberton, Cambridgeshire and can be adapted to meet the needs of other categories of trainee. It can be attached to school policies such as the one described above.

Checklist: Student Block Practice

NAME OF STUDENT _____ VALIDATING INSTITUTION _____

DATES OF PRACTICE: FROM _____ TO _____ WEEKS _____

PRELIMINARY VISITS: _____

MENTOR: _____

Preliminary   Tick

    Included in weekly bulletin _____

    Induction with head/deputy _____

    Timetable proposal at least 1 week in advance _____

    Timetable agreed at least 1 day in advance _____

                60 per cent teaching _____

                20 per cent observation _____

                20 per cent non-contact _____

    Curriculum outlines _____

    Schemes of work _____

    Homework timetable _____

    Resource materials _____

    Marking and assessment policy _____

    Recording and reporting policy _____

    Behaviour management policy _____

    Language and learning support _____

    Rewards and sanctions _____

    Equal opportunities (race and gender) _____

    Staff handbook _____

    Plan of the school _____

    School calendar _____

    Observe some lessons _____

    Meet colleagues: deputy/head _____

                  deputy _____

              deputy   _____
              teacher tutor   _____
              mentor   _____
              departmental   _____
              head of year   _____
              ancillary staff   _____

Tour of department   _____
Domestic arrangements (tea, locker, facilities, etc.)   _____
Special project agreed   _____

Practice

Included in staff diary   _____
Introduced at staff briefing   _____
Introduction to classes   _____
Written evaluations, minimum 1 week   _____
Lesson preparations, minimum 1 week + mentor   _____
Team teaching   _____
Invite teacher tutor/head/deputy to lesson   _____
Mentor and teacher tutor review weekly   _____
Draft report discussed; mentor, student and teacher tutor   _____
Report finalised   _____
Interim report   _____
Final report   _____

Wider school experience

Attached to tutor group for registration and PSE   _____
Break duty   _____
Dinner duty   _____
Extra curricular activities   _____
Parental contact   _____
Pro-active strategies   _____

Professional role

Department meetings   _____
Year meetings   _____
Staff meetings   _____
Curriculum groups   _____
PTA   _____
Observe other subjects, 1 week   _____
Shadow staff   _____
Observe other students   _____
Assemblies   _____
Governing body   _____

Final teaching practice; students to arrange interviews
    Administration   _____
    Budget/LMS   _____
    Pastoral – other years   _____
               EWS   _____
    Other outside agencies   _____
    Curriculum   _____
    Language and learning support   _____
    SEN code of practice   _____
    School visits   _____
    NQTs   _____
    Application forms and CVs   _____

Student's comments to help future students _____

_____

_____

_____

Date _____

PLEASE RETURN TO _____

APPENDIX 5: MODULES WHICH CAN BE ADDED TO CHECK-LIST ACCORDING TO CATEGORY OF TRAINEE

It should be made clear who is responsible for issuing, following up and filing the checklist, whether this be the teacher tutor, line manager or first-line supervisor/ mentor. According to status, new colleagues will need access to different aspects of school organisation. These would include:

- Tours of the library, general office and media resources areas
- Access to reprographic facilities
- Knowledge of outside agencies and referral procedures
- Knowledge specific to the school and its local communities
- Class lists
- Staff lists
- Important names, addresses, telephone and fax numbers in the LEA
- A list of other schools in the LEA
- School prospectus
- Lesson observation pro forma
- Standard forms used in the school/internal communications
- Negotiated calendar of line management meetings
- Programme of school-based induction
- Programme of LEA induction and in-service training
- Programme of meetings with peer group
- Job description
- School management and consultation structure with names of post-holders
- School development plan
- Negotiated programme of lesson observation and debriefing
- Liaison arrangements
- Appraisal policy.

APPENDIX 6: MODEL JOB DESCRIPTION FOR PROFESSIONAL TUTOR

JOB DESCRIPTION _____ SCALE: _____

PROFESSIONAL TUTOR
Reporting to: (Head Teacher)

A. You are required to carry out the duties of a school teacher as set out in the school teachers' Pay and Conditions Document (attached).

B. Your current post requires you to teach _____ to pupils in the secondary age range in the _____ cluster.

C. You are required to participate in the development of appropriate syllabuses, materials and schemes of work.

D. General duties:
    a. To carry out a share of supervisory duties in accordance with published rostas.
    b. To participate in appropriate meetings with parents and colleagues relating to the above.

E. In addition you will receive – responsibility points for which you will be a member of the senior management team. You will be expected to carry out the following specific duties, some of which may be delegated:

    1. **PURPOSE OF JOB:** To co-ordinate all training of teachers within the school. This includes initial training, induction, in-service training and ongoing professional development.
    2. Liaise with teacher training institutions on the placement of students on teaching practice in consultation with the head, governors and heads of department and faculty.
    3. Ensure that the placement of student teachers in subject areas is co-ordinated to best meet the needs of the school and the training institution.
    4. Liaise with heads of subjects to ensure that the school experience of student, licensed and newly qualified teachers is consistent and effective and in line with school policies.
    5. Co-ordinate the induction and assessment of student, licensed and newly qualified teachers.
    6. Co-ordinate the effective communication of information relating to training to all parties who 'need to know'.
    7. To have over-sight of the work and development of all subject mentors and supervisors within the school.

8. Liaise with the LEA on all matters relating to the induction, development and assessment of newly qualified teachers.

9. To be responsible for the INSET budget according to the school development plan and budget cycle, to monitor expenditure and to keep all related records. These records are subject to audit.

10. To keep a central library of information relating to in-service training courses within the LEA and by other agencies and ensure that this information is disseminated.

11. To co-ordinate the inclusion of teachers on in-service training courses according to the school development plan and identified needs.

12. To build links with other agencies who deliver in-service training including the LEA, private consultants and higher education, having regard for quality and cost effectiveness.

13. To ensure that the school's and the authority's equal opportunities policies and all other whole-school policies are promoted in the delivery of all training.

14. To have over-sight of the planning of all school-based training including the five professional days and to ensure that effective consultation takes place.

15. To raise awareness within the whole school of the training policy.

16. To keep records on all INSET in accordance with Ofsted requirements

SELECTION CRITERIA (please address these criteria in your application form and interview).

1. Successful recent experience at a managerial level in a comprehensive school. This should include having responsibility for some aspect of the training of teachers.

2. A detailed working knowledge of the legislation and framework of the education system and of new developments across the whole curriculum.

3. The ability and commitment to deliver whole-school policies across the school and to enable others to do so.

4. Oral skills: the ability to address individuals and different groups – governors, staff, pupils and parents as well as outside agencies.

5. Written skills: the ability to present papers and materials which are accessible to a wide range of individuals and groups.

6. A commitment to the school's and the authority's equal opportunities policies.

7. The ability to build and lead a team across a range of subject areas, and to be a team member. This would include having regard to the needs of all the subject and individual interests.

8. A proven record of successful innovation in a whole-school context.

9. Proven managerial and administrative skills.
10. The ability to manage a large budget.

Prepared by

APPENDIX 7: MODEL JOB DESCRIPTION FOR SUBJECT MENTOR

JOB DESCRIPTION ———————— SCALE: ————————

SUBJECT MENTOR
Reporting to:

Sections A to D of standard job description given in paragraph 4.2 of Part 1.

E. In addition you will be a subject mentor in the ———— department.

PURPOSE OF JOB
1. To provide professional support to students or new teachers in your department in voluntary partnership with that person and with others such as trainers, heads of department and senior management team with particular reference to classroom teaching skills. To have an overview of that person's professional development.
2. To coach, guide, counsel, advise and assist students and new teachers in your department.
3. To be a source of information for trainees about subject content, teaching methods, training issues, school procedures.
4. To assess the needs of the trainee and from that assessment plan jointly a training programme which includes a teaching programme, the preparation of lessons and programme of meetings, observation and visits.
5. To facilitate the trainee's access to information, schemes of work, school policies, other personnel, knowledge of pupils of a range of ages and abilities, teaching accommodation and resources.
6. To remove any constraints which hinder the trainee in following the training programme and/or developing their teaching skills. This may involve negotiation with others.
7. To be involved, in partnership with others, in the formative and summative assessment of that trainee's teaching performance and to enable him/her to evaluate and reflect upon their own performance.
8. To attend training relating to your own role as a mentor.

SELECTION CRITERIA
The successful candidate will:
1. Be a teacher with recent and relevant experience of at least one year.
2. Be able to demonstrate up-to-date knowledge and expertise in the content of their subject.
3. Be able to demonstrate knowledge and use of a variety of teaching methods and to enable others to use them.

4. Be able to demonstrate an active interest in pursuing their own professional development.
5. Be able to work collaboratively in various teams as a voluntary partner.
6. Be able to communicate effectively with a variety of individuals and groups.
7. Be committed to the promotion of equal opportunities through teaching and training.
8. Have interpersonal skills which enable others to relate to them as a guide, counsellor and assessor.
9. To be able to identify and help others to identify and reflect upon good practice in classroom teaching (their own and that of others).
10. Have a knowledge of evaluation and assessment techniques including self-assessment for teachers and pupils.
11. Be able to organise their own time and that of others.

Prepared by:
Date:

APPENDIX 8: LINE MANAGEMENT AGENDA

Question 1.   What aspects of your work are you pleased with?

Question 2.   What aspects of your work are you concerned about?

Question 3.   What have you done to raise achievement since we last met?
Work with pupils and staff can be mentioned against a checklist, eg, examining sets of books, observing lessons, monitoring school policies, checking attendance, meetings with teachers, etc.

Question 4.   Do you have any feedback for me as your line manager. What have I done that helps or hinders you?

Question 5.   What INSET/staff development has been undertaken since we last met?
a) yourself
b) your team

Question 6.   What issues have arisen out of your own line management meetings?

Question 7.   What are your targets for the future?

APPENDIX 9: LIST OF IMPORTANT ABILITIES (OXFORDSHIRE INTERNSHIP SCHEME)
(See also Appendix 11)

Section 1: Lesson planning and evaluation
1.1 Plans both individual and sequences of lessons thoroughly and appropriately.
1.2 Considers how lessons are to be evaluated and regularly engages in lesson evaluation.
1.3 Takes account of lesson evaluation in future planning and teaching.

Section 2: Classroom interactions
These are presented as a list of effects you should be trying to achieve in your classroom. Movement from phase 1 to phase 2 of the course will depend upon whether or not you are generally able to achieve these effects.

2.1 Pupils' level of talk/movement in the classroom are appropriate to the learning activity.
2.2 Pupils are attentive when this is appropriate.
2.3 Pupils are engaged in beginnings and endings of lessons which are clearly defined and orderly.
2.4 Pupils change activities smoothly within and between different phases of the lesson.
2.5 Pupils understand what they are supposed to be doing and how to do it in different phases of the lesson.
2.6 Pupils understand what the work is about.
2.7 Pupils are aware of their progress and achievements.
2.8 Pupils are positively engaged in the lesson.
2.9 Pupils are working co-operatively with each other and the teacher.
2.10 Pupils are involved in dialogue with each other and with the teacher where appropriate.
2.11 Pupils have access to the necessary resources and understand how to use them.
2.12 Pupils are working in a safe environment.

Section 3: Professional qualities
These are presented as a list of attributes which would be expected of a teacher considered as a member of a school staff.

3.1 Recognised by colleagues in school as someone with whom they can collaborate on a professional basis.
3.2 Learns from the observation of, and discussion with, colleagues and from personal experience and reflection.

141

3.3 Is ready to accept advice/criticism.
3.4 Takes part in normal pastoral and tutorial commitments.
3.5 Is punctual and reliable.

APPENDIX 10: DOMAINS FOR TEACHING COMPETENCE

HEADING	ALSO KNOWN AS OR INCLUDING
Subject knowledge	Expertise, content and teaching methods, working as part of a team, competence in delivery drawing on a range of strategies.
The national framework	Including the National Curriculum, LMS, appraisal, links with industry, SEN code of practice, Ofsted.
Cross-curricular themes	Information technology, health education, industrial awareness, environmental education, race and gender issues, economic awareness.
Evaluation, assessment and recording	Of pupil work: record keeping, National Curriculum assessment, public exam work, reporting to pupils, parents and colleagues, thorough and constructive marking, identifying current levels of pupil attainment.
Pastoral and administrative	The work of the tutor, guidance and advice, assemblies, registration, break duties, supervision, record keeping, moral and spiritual wellbeing of pupils.
The professional role	Meetings, whole-school matters, understanding and participating in school life, cover, attendance and punctuality, appearance, school structures, LEA structures, school community, legal and contractual framework, effective professional relationships.
Planning, preparation and subject application	Knowing how pupils learn, setting appropriate objectives for children of different ages and abilities, drawing on previous work, planning and organisation, differentiation, flexibility, setting and marking class work and homework, use of a planning framework, curriculum of individual lessons and in a sequence, progression, development of pupils' language and communication skills.
Communication/ interaction	Relationships (with pupils, staff and others), rapport, class control, discipline, promoting a healthy environment, manner and projection, personal qualities, sensitivity to individual needs and differences, explaining, questioning attitudes.
Classroom management and teaching skills	Delivery, orderly environment for learning, resources development and management, teaching performance, promotion of learning, varying activities, beginnings and endings, groupings, rewards and sanctions.
Inner city issues	Equal opportunities, ESL, disruptive behaviour, low expectations, absenteeism, language issues.

Reflection	Observation, evaluation of own performance, phase knowledge, transitions, participation in training, reviewing methods of teaching and programmes of work.
Management/ Further professional development	Select, appoint and train teachers, induct NQTs, review development and management of school functions, manage support staff, carry out administration tasks including ordering and allocating resources.

APPENDIX 11: LIST OF IMPORTANT ABILITIES (SECTION 2: CLASSROOM INTERACTION)
(See also Appendix 9)

This section of the list is expressed in terms of effects to achieve in the classroom.

2.1   • Expectations are made clear.
     • Expectations are consistently enforced by:
        taking disciplinary action;
        using non-verbal clues;
        constantly monitoring behaviour in the classroom.

2.2   • Expectations are made clear about appropriate behaviour when either the teacher or pupil is addressing the class or group.
     • Speaks with a clear and distinct voice which is pitched appropriately.
     • Expectations are consistently enforced.

2.3   • Expectations are made clear.
     • Attention of pupils is gained before starting the lesson.

2.4   • It is clearly explained to the whole class or to individuals when appropriate how and when to move on to a new task.
     • Movement is managed as necessary.

2.5   • Secures pupils' attention before instructions are given.
     • Instructions are clear and language is pitched appropriately.

2.6   • Basic concepts and skills are explained competently using appropriate language.
     • Progress of pupils is monitored and help is given to both individuals and groups.

2.7   • Pupils are given regular positive oral and written feedback on their work.
     • The objectives of particular work and the basis on which it is assessed are made clear.
     • Some element of self-evaluation is encouraged.

2.8   • There is a variety of stimulating activities and materials.
     • Activities are timed to allow maximum pupil concentration.
     • Progress of pupils is monitored and help is given to both individuals and groups.
     • Praise and encouragement are used.
     • Teacher communicated enthusiasm for the learning activities and subject matter.

2.9
- Teacher shows respect for the pupils and their views.
- Appropriate use of praise, encouragement and disciplinary action.
- Appropriate activities and groupings are used to encourage pupils to work together.

2.10
- Effective use of pupil names.
- Questioning skills, eg, rephrasing and reinforcing pupil answers are used to encourage a dialogue and involve *all* pupils.
- Activities allow pupils to talk to each other about the concepts being learnt.

2.11
- Equipment and materials are available and distributed at the appropriate time.
- Resources are appropriate to the pupil's age and ability including language and presentation.

2.12
- Hazards and procedures are explained, eg, in the use of dangerous equipment or behaviour out of school.

APPENDIX 12: LESSON OBSERVATION EVALUATION SHEET

DATE _____ Class: _____ Subject: _____

Teacher:

Observer:

(This evaluation sheet should be accompanied by a lesson script indicating exactly how the time was spent by teacher and pupils).

Resources used (please tick)

Worksheets	Text books
Additional reference books	Overhead projector
Video	Information technology
Tape/cassette recorders	Pictures/visuals
Objects to handle	Blackboard
Other (please specify):	

Was there a support teacher in the room?

THE LEARNING ENVIRONMENT

1. Does the teacher take most of his/her lessons in this room?   YES/NO

2. In a normal week, how many other members of staff teach in this room?
   ONE/MORE THAN ONE

3. Was the environment safe and all potential hazards explained?   YES/NO

4. Were any wall charts or other visual aids on view round the room?   YES/NO

5. Was any work by pupils displayed in the room?   YES/NO

6. Was display presented in an attractive way, ie, carefully mounted, lettering neatly done, mistakes corrected and work dated?   YES/NO

7. Was the room tidy when the class arrived and when they left?   YES/NO

8. Were desks and chairs arranged in a manner conducive to good concentration, good listening and a clear view of the blackboard or screen?   YES/NO

Comments on learning environment:

PREPARATION

1. Were all the materials and resources required for the lesson ready in the room?   YES/NO

   Except for:

   (How was this obtained?)

2. Were all tape, video and IT resources ready for use at the correct point?   YES/NO

3. Were lesson plans available?   YES/NO

4. How were any support staff enabled to participate in the lesson?
   a. Working with individuals.?
   b. Working with groups?
   c. Working with the whole class?
   d. Evidence of liaison?
   e. Other comments:

5. Had differentiated work been prepared in readiness for the lesson?   YES/NO

   If 'yes', how?

6. Was homework set?   YES/NO

Define the homework task:

7. Had pupils' previous work been marked?   YES/NO

8. Were constructive comments used in marking?   YES/NO

9. Were the teacher's records up to date?   YES/NO

Comments on preparation:

ORGANIZATION

1. Was there a set procedure for entering and leaving the room?   YES/NO

2. Was the teacher in the room to receive the class as they arrived?   YES/NO

3. If not, what was the reason for late arrival?

4. Were books, folders, worksheets, etc. ready on the desks for use?   YES/NO

5. If not, were these given out and later collected in a controlled and speedy fashion?   YES/NO

6. Was a register taken?   YES/NO

7. Were pupils encouraged to sit in mixed race, gender and ability groups?   YES/NO

Comments on organization:

CONTENT

1. Did the teacher relate the work to what had been done previously?   YES/NO

2. If so, how was it done?
   Teacher explained
   Questioning techniques
   Both
   Other (please specify)

3. Was the subject of the lesson the beginning of a new project?   YES/NO

4. If so, was the whole project explained to the class before they began this part of it?   YES/NO

5. Did the class understand the aim of the lesson?   YES/NO

6. Was the subject matter suitable for this age group?   YES/NO

7. If the subject matter was unsuitable was this because it was
   Too difficult
   Too easy
   Suitable for younger/older pupils
   Presented in an unsuitable way
   Materials were unsuitable

8. Was there a good balance between teacher and pupil activity?   YES/NO

9. Were the pupils sufficiently interested?   YES/NO

10. What provision did the teacher make for slow learners or children not fluent in English to make the lesson accessible? (Please specify).

11. What provision did the teacher make for the more able in order to:
    a. Give additional information?

    b. Set higher level work including questioning?

    c. Set extra work?

12. Did the teacher appear to have control of the subject matter?

Comments on content:

PRESENTATION

1. Were overhead transparencies clearly printed and legible from all angles of the room?　YES/NO

2. Was the blackboard clean at the start of the lesson with the date and title neatly and legibly written on it?　YES/NO

3. Was the teacher's blackboard work clearly written so that it could be read from all parts of the room by all children?　YES/NO

Comments on presentation:

CLASS CONTROL/RELATIONSHIPS WITH PUPILS

1. Did the teacher gain the pupils' attention before beginning the lesson?
   YES/NO

2. Did the teacher insist on complete quiet while s/he was speaking?　YES/NO

3. Did the teacher use language with which the children were familiar?
   YES/NO

4. Did the teacher appear too familiar with the children?　YES/NO

5. Did the teacher appear too distant and talk down to the pupils?　YES/NO

6. Did the teacher insist on children putting their hands up to answer and seek assistance?　YES/NO

7. Were questions used to involve all pupils including non-volunteers?
   YES/NO

8. Did the teacher use a variety of questioning techniques encouraging different forms of response?
   Oral work:　　　　　YES/NO
   Written work:　　　　YES/NO

9. Did the teacher use clear explanations?   YES/NO

10. How did the teacher deal with minor disturbances/interruptions/setbacks?

11. Was the teacher's speech
     Too loud
     Too soft
     Too fast
     Good
     Monotonous

12. Did the teacher make positive use of non-verbal communication, eg, signalling, body language, personal appearance, eye contact?   YES/NO

13. Did the teacher give praise when appropriate?   YES/NO

14. Did the teacher help individuals as needed?   YES/NO

15. Did the teacher move around the room to ascertain where help was needed?   YES/NO/OCCASIONALLY

16. Were pupils kept waiting too long for help?   YES/NO

17. While helping individuals was the teacher aware of the situation in the rest of the classroom?   MOST OF THE TIME/SELDOM/NO

18. Did the class on the whole appear to enjoy the lesson?   YES/NO

19. Did the teacher appear to enjoy the lesson?   YES/NO

Comments on class control and relationships:

OVERALL HOW WOULD YOU RATE:

	Good	Satisfactory	Unsatisfactory
Class control			
Teaching techniques			
Pupil learning			
Pupil activity			

Please return to:

Bibliography

Abrams, F (1991) 'Articled staff project collapsing', *TES*, 21 June.

Adult Literacy and Basic Skills Unit (1988) *The Certificate in Teaching Basic Communication Skills. A handbook*, London.

Anderson, E M and Lucasse Shannon, A (1988) 'Toward a conceptualization of mentoring'. *Journal of Teacher Education*, Jan – Feb, pp 38–42.

Andrews, R and Protherough, R. (1989) 'The figure at the back: teaching practice supervision', in George, N and Protherough, R *Supervision in Education*, 39, University of Hull Institute of Education.

Austin, G and Reynolds, D (1990) 'Managing for improved school effectiveness', *School Organization*, 10, pp 2–3.

Barrett, E, Barton, L, Furlong, J, Galvin, C, Miles, S. and Whitty, G (1992) 'New routes to qualified teacher status', *Cambridge Journal of Education*, 22(3), pp 323–6.

Barth, R S (1991) *Improving Schools from Within: Teachers, parents and principals can make the difference*, San Francisco and Oxford: Jossey Bass.

Bassey, M (1991) 'All right in theory but short on time', *TES*, 29 March.

Beardon, T, Booth, M, Hargreaves, D and Reiss, M (1992) 'School-led initial teacher training: The way forward', *Cambridge Education Papers*, No 2, Cambridge.

Benton, P (ed.) (1990) *The Oxford Internship Scheme. Integration and Partnership in Initial Teacher Education*, London: Calouste Gulbenkian Foundation.

Berrill, M (1990) *A Foundation for Excellence. A mentoring approach to the development of basic teaching proficiency*, Luton: Challney Community College.

Berrill, M (1991) *A Foundation for Excellence. A structured approach to mentoring and the development of basic teaching proficiency*, Luton: Challney Community College.

Bines, H and Welton, J (eds) (1995) *Managing Partnership in Teacher Training and Development*, London: Routledge.

Blake, D (1990) 'The teacher training debate: some parallels from health and social work', *Journal of Education Policy*, 5, 4.

Booth, M, Furlong, J and Wilkin, M (1990) *Partnership in Initial Teacher Training*, London: Cassell.

Broadhead, P (1986) 'A blueprint for the Good Teacher? The HMI/DES model of good primary practice', *British Journal of Educational Studies*, XXXV, 1, pp 57–71.

Bush, T, Glatter, R *et al.* (1980) *Approaches to School Management*, Oxford: OUP.

Calderhead, J (1988) 'Learning from introductory school experience', *Journal of Education for Teaching*, 14, 1.

Calderhead, J (1992) 'Induction: A Research perspective on the professional growth of the NQT', General Teaching Council (England and Wales) and NFER, Slough.

Cameron-Jones, M (1991) 'Training Teachers. A practical guide', Scottish Council for Research in Education, practitioner mini-paper, 10.

CATE (1992) *The Accreditation of Initial Teacher Training under Circulars 9/92 and 35/92*, London: CATE.

CATE (1994) *Profiles of Competence, Draft, Notes of Guidance*, London: CATE.

City and Guilds London Institute (1990–91) '7307 – Further and Adult Education Teacher's certificate', London: CGLI.

City & Guilds London Institute (undated) Unpublished consultative document: 'City and Guilds 7307. A competence based certificate for further and Adult Education teachers', London: CGLI.

Clarke, K (1992) *Speech to North of England Education Conference*, January 4.

CNAA (1989) 'Mentorship: Notes on mentorship within CNAA approved courses of inservice training for teachers in further education'. London: CNAA.

CNAA (1991) 'Competence-based approaches to teacher education: viewpoints and issues', Paper TEA/91/30, London: CNAA.

CNAA (undated) Committee for teacher education: 'The assessment of Professional practice'. London: CNAA.

CTC Trust and DFE (1994) The CTC Smallpeice Programme. School Centred Initial Teacher Training in Technology and Science. London: CTC Trust.

Collins, N (1986) *New Teaching Skills*, Oxford: Oxford University Press.

Dale, F and Robinson, A (1988) 'Framework for Teaching. Readings for the intending secondary teacher'. EP228, Milton Keynes: Open University.

Deas, R *et al.* (1989) 'Roles and relationships in Teaching Practice', University of Sheffield Division of Education, publication 12.

Dent, H C (1975) *The Training of Teachers in England and Wales 1800–1975*, London: Hodder and Stoughton.

DES (1972) *Teacher Education and Training. A report by the Committee of Enquiry appointed by the Secretary of State for Education and Science, under the Chairmanship of Lord James of Rusholme* (The James Report) London: HMSO.

DES (1982) 'The new teacher in school', in *Matters for Discussion*, 15 an HMI series, London: HMSO.

DES (1983) *White Paper: Teaching Quality*, CMND 8836, London: HMSO.

DES (1984) *Initial Teacher Training: Approval of Courses*, Circular 3/84 London: DES.

DES (1987) *Quality in schools: The Initial Training of Teachers*, an HMI survey Jan 1983–Jan 1985, London: HMSO.

DES (1988a) 'Initial teacher training in universities in England, Northern Ireland and Wales', *Education Observed*, 7, London: HMSO.

DES (1988b) *The Education Reform Act*, London: HMSO.

DES (1989a) *The Education (Teachers) Regulations*, Circular 18/89, London: HMSO.

DES (1989b) *Initial Teacher Training: Approval of courses*, Circular 24/89, London: HMSO.

DES (1989c) *Initial Teacher Training in France. The training of secondary teachers in the Academie de Toulouse*, a paper by HMI, London: HMSO.

DES (1989d) *Teacher supply in 17 schools in Tower Hamlets and Wandsworth*, a report by HMI, London: HMSO.

DES (1989e) *Schoolteacher Appraisal: A National Framework. Report of the National Steering Group on the School Teacher Appraisal Pilot Study*, London: HMSO.

DES (1989f) *Perspectives on Teacher Education. Other trainers' views*, a report by HMI, London: HMSO.

DES (1989g) *The Provisional Teacher Program in New Jersey*, a paper by HMI, London: HMSO.

DES (1989h) *The Renewed Teaching Experience Scheme at Trent Polytechnic Nottingham*, a report by HMI, London: HMSO.

DES (1990a) *Developing School Management. The way forward*, School Management Task Force, London: HMSO.

DES (1990b) *Hertfordshire Action on Teacher Supply/Mature Entrants' Teacher Training Scheme*, a report by HMI, June 1987 – May 1988 and October 1989 – March 1990, London: HMSO.

DES (1990c) 'The Treatment and Assessment of Probationary Teachers', (Admin. memorandum 1/90), London: HMSO.

DES (1990d) *Schools in Hackney: some issues*, a report by HMI, London: HMSO.

DES (1991a) *The Education (Schools) Bill*, London: HMSO.

DES (1991b) *European Community Teachers in the London Borough of Havering*, A report by HMI, September 1989–July 1990, London: HMSO.

DES (1991c) *Training teachers for Inner City Schools*, a report by HMI, 10 October 1989–31 March 1990, London: HMSO.

DES (1991d) *The Parent's Charter. You and your child's education*, London: HMSO.

DES (1991e) 'Revision of the Education (teachers) Regulations 1989', Letter, 27 March, to all LEAs in England and Wales, all grant-maintained schools, all non-maintained special schools, all teacher associations.

DES (1991f) 'Schoolteacher Probation', Letter, 17 September, to CEOs and others for consultation.

DES (1992) *The Induction and Probation of New Teachers*, a report by HMI, London: HMSO.

Development Dimension International (1984) *Utilizing Effective Disciplinary Action and Key Principles*.

DFE (1992a) *Initial Teacher Training, Secondary phase*, Circular 9/92, London: HMSO.

DFE (1992b) *Choice and Diversity* White Paper, London: HMSO.

DFE (1992c) Administrative memorandum 2//92 'Induction of Newly Qualified Teachers', London: HMSO.

DFE (1993a) *Education Act*, London: HMSO.

DFE (1993b) *Gout. Proposals for the Reform of Initial Teacher Training*, London: HMSO.

DFE (1993c) *Physical and Mental Fitness to Teach of Teachers and of Entrants to Initial Teacher Training*, Circular 13/93, London: HMSO.

DFE (1993d) School Centred Initial Teacher Training (SCITT). Letter of invitation, 5.3.93. London: DFE.

DFE (1994a) *School Teachers' Pay and Conditions Document 1994*, London: HMSO.

DFE (1994b) *Education Act*, London: HMSO.

DFE (1994c) Statutory Instrument 1994 no 222, 'The Registered Teachers' Scheme', London: HMSO.

Earley, P (1992) *Beyond Initial Teacher Training: Induction and the role of the LEA*, Slough: NFER.

Egan, G (1982, 1986) *The Skilled Helper*, (2nd and 3rd edns) London: Brooks Cole.

Elliott, J (1976) 'Preparing teachers for classroom accountability', *Education for Teaching*, 100, 49–71.

Farrell, M (1991) 'Possible course structure'. Distance Education for Teaching, London: South Bank Polytechnic.

Fieman-Neuser, S, Parker, M B and Zeichner, K (1990) 'Are Mentor Teachers Teacher Educators?' Paper to the American Educational Research Association. Boston: National Center for Research on Teacher Education, Michigan State University.

Fullan, M G (1986) 'The Management of Change', in *World Year Book of Education 1986 – The Management of Schools*, London: Kogan Page.

Furlong, V J, Hirst, P, Pocklington, K and Miles, S (1988) *Initial Teacher Training and the Role of the School* Milton Keynes: Open University Press.

Furlong, V J and Maynard, T (1995) *Mentoring Student Teachers: The Growth of Professional Knowledge*, London: Routledge.

'The Supply of Teachers for the 1990s', Government response to the 2nd report from the Education, Science and Arts Committee, session 1989–90, presented by the Secretary of State to Parliament, London: HMSO.

Handy, C (1988) 'Cultural forces in schools', in Glatter, R *et al. Understanding School Management*, Buckingham: Open University Press.

Hansard (1991) Parliamentary debates, 4 November, 198, 3, 240–2, 292–4, 300.

Hargreaves, D (1990a) 'Out of BEd and into practice', *TES*, 8 September.

Hargreaves, D (1990b) 'Judge radicals by results'. *TES*, 6 October.

Hargreaves, D and Hopkins, D (1991) *The Empowered School*, London: Cassell.

Hargreaves, D, Hopkins, D *et al.* (1989) *Planning for School Development*, London: DES.

Hartwood Futrell, M 'Selecting and compensating mentor teachers: a win-win scenario', *Theory into practice*, xxvii, 3, pp 223–5.

Hertfordshire Education Department (1991) 'Criteria for the assessment of teachers,' (Licensed teachers/DM), Hertford: Hertfordshire Education Department.

Hextall, I *et al.* (1991) 'Imaginative projects. Arguments for a new teacher education'. London: Goldsmiths College.

HMI (1988) *The New Teacher in School*, London: HMSO.

HMI (1992) *School-based Initial Teacher Training in England and Wales: A Report by HM Inspectorate*, London: HMSO.

Hillgate Group (1989) *Learning to Teach*, London: The Claridge Press.

Holly, P (ed.) (1991) 'Developing managers in Education. A review of management issues, current initiatives and prospects for future development in schools', Cambridge: CRAC.

Hoover, N L, O'Shea L J and Carrou R G (1988) 'Supervision. The supervisor-intern relationship and effective interpersonal communication skills', *Journal of Teacher Education*, March–April, pp 22–7.

Hopkins, D and Ainscow, M (1992) 'Aboard the "Moving School"', in *Educational Leadership*, Nov 92 pp 79–81.

Hopkins, D and Ainscow, M (1993) *Making Sense of School Improvement*, Cambridge Institute of Education.

House of Commons Education, Science and Arts Committee (Session 1989–90) 'The supply of teachers for the 1990s, 2nd committee report, 1, London: HMSO.

Hughes, M (1980) 'Reconciling professional and administrative concerns', in Bush, T. *et al.* (eds) *Approaches to School Management*, London: Harper and Row.

Hunt, I (1990) 'Teacher profiles', paper to the NAHT teacher training committee, London Borough of Newham or NAHT (Haywards Heath).

Hunt, I (1991a) 'Licensed Teacher Scheme. Exhibition meeting 24 April 1991, handout pack'. London Borough of Newham.

Hunt, I (1991b) 'Change in teacher regulations', letter to NAHT.

Hunt, I (1991c) 'Licensed Teacher Scheme. Teacher mentor training', timetable for 8 July, London Borough of Newham.

Jackson, M (1991) 'Vocational council snubbed', *TES*, 13 December.

Kagan, D M and Albertson, L M (1987) 'Student teaching: perceptions of supervisory meetings', *Journal of Education for Teaching*, 13, 1.

Kelly, M, Beck T and Thomas, J (1991) 'More than a supporting Act', *TES*, 8 November.

Kirkman, S (1990) 'What makes a good teacher?', *TES*, 7 September.

Knight, R O (1990a) 'Mature Entrants Teacher Training Scheme (HATS Project), Phase 1, Cohort 7: Polytechnic Professional Studies Course, 8 October–7 December 1990', scheme structure, assignments, management, regulations and component course syllabuses, Hatfield Polytechnic.

Kueker, J and Haensly, P (1991) 'Developing mentorship/induction year teacher dyads in a generic special education teacher training program', paper to Annual Conference of AERA, Chicago.

Lacey, C (1977) *The Socialisation of Teachers*, London: Methuen.

Lambert, J (1992) *Induction of Newly Trained and Appointed Teachers*, London: GTC (England and Wales) and Slough: NFER.

Lancaster University School of Education (1990) 'Building the Bridge: profiling the student teacher. A new approach to assessment', January, Conference proceedings.

Lawlor, S (1990) *Teachers Mistaught: Training theories or education in subjects?* London: Centre for Policy Studies.

Local Education Authorities Project (LEAP) (1991) *Appraisal in Schools. Course members book*, London: BBC.

Lodge, B (1991a) 'Pay for teaching practice', *TES*, 15 March.

Lodge, B (1991b) 'Trainers braced for shunt into classroom', *TES*, 29 March.

Lodge, B (1991c) 'Articled route "less wasteful"', (Report on speech by Michael Fallon), *TES*, 1 November.

Lodge, B (1991d) 'OU taps a rich teacher source', *TES*, 22 November.

McIntyre, D, Hagger, H, Wilkin, M (eds) (1993) *Mentoring: Perspectives on school-based teacher education*, London: Kogan Page.

McLennan, S and Seadon, T (1988) 'What price school-based work? Reflections on a school-sited PGCE method course', *Cambridge Journal of Education*, 18, 3.

McNair, A (1944) *Teachers and Youth Leaders* (The McNair Report). London: HMSO.

Mercer, D and Abbott, T (1989) 'Democratic learning in teacher education: partnership supervision in the teaching practice', *Journal of Education for Teaching*, 15, 2.

Miliband, D (1991) 'Markets, politics and education. Beyond the Education Reform Act', Institute for Public Policy Research, Education & Training Paper, 3.

Montgomery, D (1984) 'Evaluation and enhancement of teaching performance', Kingston Polytechnic.

Montgomery, D and Hadfield, N (1989) *Practical Teacher Appraisal*, London: Kogan Page.

National Commission on Education (1993) *Learning to Succeed: A radical look at education today and a strategy for the future*, report of the Paul Hamlyn Foundation National Commission on Education, London: Heinemann.

National Curriculum Council (1991) *The National Curriculum and the Initial Training of Student, Articled and Licensed Teachers*, York: NCC.

NCVQ (1990) *Occupational Standards for Managers. Management I & II*, London: NCVQ.

NCVQ (1991) *Units for Assessment and Verification. National Standards Endorsed by the Training and Development Lead Body*, London: NCVQ.

NCVQ Training and Development Lead Body (1991) *National Standards for Training and Development*, London: NCVQ.

Nevins, L and Weingart, H (1991) 'The preparation of mentors: what are the effects of training?', paper presented to AERA annual congress, Chicago.

Nias, J (1980) 'Leadership styles and job satisfaction in primary schools', in Bush, T Glatter, R *et al. Approaches to School Management*, Oxford: OUP.

Odell, S J (1986) 'Induction support of new teachers. A functional approach', *Journal of Teacher Education*, Jan–Feb, pp 26–9.

Ofsted (1993a) *The Articled Teachers' Scheme Sept 1990–July 1992*, a report from the office of HMCI, London: HMSO.

Ofsted (1993b) *The Licensed Teachers' Scheme Sept 1990–July 1992*, a report from the office of HMCI, London: HMSO.

O'Hear, A (1991) 'Getting the teachers we deserve', *Education Guardian*, 19 March.

Oldroyd, D, Smith, K and Lee, J (1984) *School based staff development activities: A handbook for secondary schools*, Harlow: Longman for the Schools Council.

Open University (1991) 'EP228. Assignment book', Milton Keynes: Open University.

Open University (1994) *Postgraduate Certificate in Education: Course Handbook for partner schools*, Milton Keynes: OU, School of Education.

Parker, G (1994) *Profiles of Teacher Competences: Consultation on draft guidance*, London: Teacher Training Agency.

Paul Hamlyn Fondation (1994) *Mentoring in Initial Teacher Education: Findings from a research initiative by the Paul Hamlyn Foundation*, London: PHF.

Perry, P (1991) 'A model for best training', *TES*, 25 October.

Pyke, N (1991) 'Phoney peace on the training front', *TES*, 11 October.

Ree, H (1973) *Educator Extraordinary. The Life and Achievements of Henry Morris*, Harlow: Longman.

Rosenholz, S (1989) *Teachers' Workplace*, New York: Longman.

RSA Examination Board (1990a) *RSA Teacher and Trainer Diploma (Management). Pilot Scheme 1990 onwards*, London: RSA.

RSA Examination Board (1990b) *Training and Development Lead Body Standards. Implications for RSA Teacher and Trainer Qualifications*, London: RSA.

Ruddock, J (1987) 'Partnership supervision as a basis for the professional development of new and experienced teachers, in Wideen, M and Andrews, I (eds) *Staff Development for School Improvement*, London: Falmer Press.

Science Teacher Education Project (1974) *Theory into Practice. Activities in School for Student Teachers*, Haysam, J. and Sutton, C. (eds), Maidenhead: McGraw-Hill.

Seriphe and Trin (1991) 'New routes for initial training of teachers: A commentary', paper presented at a conference on April 17 at the Institute of Education, University of London.

Shaw, R (1992a) 'Can mentoring raise achievement in schools?', in *Mentoring in Schools*, ed. Wilkin, London: Kogan Page.

Shaw, R (1992b) 'School based training: the view from the schools', in *Cambridge Journal of Education*, 22, 3, pp 363–75.

Shaw, R (1995) 'Developing teacher education in a secondary school', in *Managing Partnership in Teacher Training and Development*, Bines and Welton (eds), London: Routledge.

Shulman, L S (1986) 'Those who understand: knowledge growth in teaching', *Educational Researcher*, 15,2.

Stokes, A (1990) *Communication: Listening Skills*, London: Breakthrough Educational Publications.

Straw, J, Fatchett, D, Armstrong, H and Smith, A (1989) *Children First. Labour's policy for raising standards in schools*, London: Parliamentary Labour Party Education Team.

Suffolk Education Department (1987) *In the Light of Torches*, London: Industrial Society Press.

TASC (April 1990) *Back to School. A guide for teachers returning to the classroom*, London: Central Office of Information for the DES, HMSO.

Thames Polytechnic (unpublished 1990a) 'Competency statement criteria' and 'Competency assessment sheet', London: author.

Thames Polytechnic (1990b) *PGCE Secondary course. Articled Teachers' scheme. Stage 3. Teaching Practice*, London: author.

Thies Sprinthall, L (1986) 'A collaborative approach for mentor training: A working model', *Journal of Teacher Education*, Nov–Dec, pp 13–20.

Times Educational Supplement (TES) (1990) 'Happy to have an intern on the "ward"', 7 December.

TES (1991a) 'Voices of experience', 22 March.

TES (1991b) 'On the job training will replace probation year', 20 September.

TES (1991c) 'Staff slow to change', 22 November.

TES (1991d) 'Study finds training gap', 13 December.

TES (1994) 'In danger of shortfall', 3 June.

Tower Hamlets (1991) 'DES probation 1991', letters and sheets, London: author.

Understanding British Industry (1993) *Teachers' Business: A professional development programme for teachers drawing business and the community into their work*,
London: UBI.

University of Cambridge, Department of Education (1990) *Guidelines for Mentors
and Supervisors*, Cambridge: author.

University of Oxford 'List of important abilities: Section 2: Classroom interactions', Oxford: Anna Pendry.

University of Oxford 'List of important abilities. Ways of using the list', Oxford:
Anna Pendry.

University of Oxford, Department of Educational Studies (1990) *The PGCE
Course* 1990/1. Course Handbook, Oxford: author.

University of Oxford, Department of Educational Studies (undated) *Briefing
papers for Professional Tutors and Mentors*, Oxford: author.

Walker, R and Adelman, C (1975) *A Guide to Classroom Observation*, London:
Routledge.

Watts, J (1980) 'Sharing it out: the role of the head in participatory government',
in Bush, T Glatter R, *et al.*, *Approaches to School Management*, Oxford: OUP.

Wilkin, M (1990) 'The Development of Partnership in the United Kingdom' in M
Booth, J Furlong and M Wilkin (eds) *Partnership in Initial Teacher Training*,
London: Cassell.

Wilkin, M (ed.) (1992) *Mentoring in Schools*, London: Kogan Page.

Wragg, E C (1984a) *Classroom Teaching Skills. The Research Findings of the
Teacher Education Project*, London: Croom Helm.

Wragg, E C (1984b) 'Training skilful teachers: some implications for practice',
chapter 10 in Wragg, 1984a, op. cit.

Yosha, P (1991) 'Benefits of an induction program. What do mentors and novices
say?', paper presented to a symposium on 'Connecticut's commitment to the
teaching profession: A focus on induction', AERA congress, Chicago.

Zeichner, K (1990) 'Changing directions in the practicum', *Journal of Education for
Teaching*, 16, 2.

Zeichner, K *et al.* (1990) 'Are mentor teachers teacher educators?', paper presented
to the American Education Research Association, Boston.

Zimpher, N L and Rieger S R 'Mentoring teachers: What are the issues?', *Theory
into Practice*, xxvii, 3, pp 175–82.

Index